SO SEND I YOU

WORKMEN OF GOD

P U B L I S H E R S
BOX 3566 · GRAND RAPIDS. MI 49501

*PUBLISHING BOOKS THAT FEED
THE SOUL WITH THE WORD OF GOD.*

CHRISTIAN LITERATURE CRUSADE
Fort Washington, Pennsylvania 19034

SO SEND I YOU

WORKMEN OF GOD

OSWALD CHAMBERS

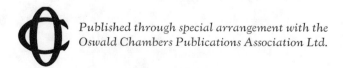

Published through special arrangement with the
Oswald Chambers Publications Association Ltd.

Discovery House Publishers is affiliated with Radio Bible Class,
Grand Rapids, Michigan

Discovery House books are distributed to the trade by Thomas Nelson
Publishers, Nashville, Tennessee 37214

Library of Congress Cataloging-in-Publication Data

Chambers, Oswald, 1874–1917.
  [So send I you]
  So send I you, and, Workmen of God / Oswald Chambers.
      p. cm.
  ISBN 0-929239-74-1
  1. Missionaries—Appointment, call, and election.
2. Missionaries—Religious life. 3. Pastoral theology. 4. Clergy—Office.
I. Chambers, Oswald, 1874–1917. Workmen of God.
II. Title. III. Title: Workmen of God.
BV2063.C45 1993
253—dc20   93–395
                                                                                          CIP

CONTENTS

PUBLISHER'S FOREWORD

It has been five years since Discovery House began issuing new editions of the works of Oswald Chambers. Largely unknown to the present generation of readers, they are being increasingly appreciated by those who take their faith seriously—those who seek insights into scriptural truths because of their passion for God and His Word. You who take the time to read Chambers will find, as the great missions leader Samuel Zwemer suggested in his foreword to the first edition of *So Send I You,* that his "words pulsate with life and are a clarion call away from idle dreams to the stern path of duty."

The publisher commends *So Send I You* and *Workmen of God* to you as some of Oswald Chambers' finest work. Many have requested that we reissue these books because of their timelessness in encouraging and directing those who feel called to vocational Christian service. In a real sense, all believers are called to serve. Chambers enjoins us to reject the self-centered, narcissistic bent of a generation that seeks fulfillment in doing "what is best for me" and to find the fulfillment which God alone can give to His sons and daughters who in sacrifice and obedience seek His will above all else.

Oswald Chambers died in 1917 in the Egyptian desert, having served less than two decades in formal ministry. Because he lived the life of a workman of God we, at the end of the twentieth century, are heirs of his rich spiritual legacy. By the grace of God he continues to speaks to our hungry hearts.

THE PUBLISHER

FOREWORD TO SO SEND I YOU

A preface or foreword is scarcely needed to introduce the reader to this treasure-house of thought on missions. Those who have read other books by our friend, Oswald Chambers, know what to expect—a message not for superficial minds and hearts. Those who love to think on the kingdom and whose heart the King has entered will not be disappointed as they read these pages.

These stirring talks were given to the students at the Bible training College in London, of which the Reverend Oswald Chambers was principal before he went out to Egypt. The students that heard him are now scattered in many parts of the world, and proving faithful witnesses of Christ.

The twenty-two short chapters are in a sense Bible studies, but they are not mere Bible readings—strings of texts with a moral. They whisper the secret of the burning heart, of the fully surrendered life, of a love that will not let go. The words pulsate with life and are a clarion-call away from idle daydreams to the stern path of duty. One sentence, among many others, specially riveted my attention and sums up the style, the man, and the message:

"In my study am I wool-gatherer,
or like one looking for my Lord?"

This book will not find casual readers, but the thoughtful reader will want to read it a second time and God will bless the message.

S. M. Zwemer
Princeton, N.J.

FOREWORD TO WORKMEN OF GOD

Another book by Oswald Chambers! I wonder if his eager readers think of him as a writer of mature old age, giving the stored wisdom of a long life in these searching, virile, helpful messages. If so, they are mistaken. The facts are that his books are records of addresses and lectures that he gave during a decade of wonderful public and private ministry both to students and congregations who were privileged to listen to him between 1907 and 1917. His wife, with God-given wisdom and energy, garnered this precious treasure by taking verbatim reports in shorthand throughout these busy years. Thus, when Oswald Chambers suddenly and unexpectedly died in Egypt in his early forties (during the Great War), he left behind him a wealth of spiritual vitamins, which have ever since been enriching us through his books.

And now this latest book goes forth at a time when soul-sickness is more than ever rampant. The messages are full of spiritual discernment and diagnosis, and they were first given at Speke Hall, Battersea, when Oswald Chambers was Principal of the Bible Training College at Clapham Common. Those of us who listened to him then, and worked with him, will never forget his forceful, challenging statements, and we can never be thankful enough for the inspiration of his life and the blessing that resulted from his teaching.

He had a brilliant intellect, a highly trained disciplined mind and body, and an outstanding gift for teaching; but his great power lay in his consuming devotion to his Lord, in his entire reliance on the Holy Spirit, and in his absolute trust in the revelation of God through the Scriptures.

As these messages now go forth to a still wider circle, may they continually cause many to be wise in winning souls.

Mary R. Hooker
Ridgelands College, Wimbledon
April 1937

SO SEND I YOU

The Call

The voice of the nature of God—"Also I heard the voice of the Lord, saying: 'Whom shall I send, and who will go for Us?' Then I said, 'Here am I! Send me' " —Isaiah 6:8.

When we speak of a call we nearly always leave out one essential feature: the nature of the one who calls. We speak of the call of the sea, the call of the mountains, the call of the great ice barriers. These calls are heard by a few only because the call is the expression of the nature from which the call comes, and can only be heard by those who are attuned to that nature.

The call of God is essentially expressive of the nature of God; it is His own voice. Paul says that "God demonstrates His own love toward us" (Rom. 5:8), the love that is exactly expressive of His nature. Get that thought with regard to the call of God. Very few of us hear the call of God because we are not in the place to answer; the call does not communicate because we have not the nature of the One who is calling. In the case of Isaiah, his soul was so attuned because of the tremendous crisis he had passed through, that the call of God was recorded to his amazed soul. God did not lay a strong compulsion on Isaiah. Isaiah was in the presence of God and he overheard, as it were, the soliloquy of God: "Whom shall I send, and who will go for Us?" and in conscious freedom he replied, "Here am I! Send me."

There is a good deal of instruction in watching the faces of people in certain surroundings—by the sea shore, in an art gallery, during music. You can tell at once if they are listening to the call of the thing or simply reflecting themselves. Most of us have no ear for anything but ourselves, anything that is not me we cannot hear. We are dead to and without interest in the finest music; we can yawn in a picture gallery and be uninspired by a sunrise or a sunset. That is true not only of the soul's denseness to natural beauties, or to music and art and literature, but true with regard to the awakening of the soul to the call of God. To be brought within the zone of God's voice is to be profoundly altered.

The call of God is not the echo of my nature, but expresses God's nature. The call of God does not consider my affinities or personality. It is a call that I cannot hear as long as I consider my personality or temperament. But as soon as I am brought into the condition Isaiah was in, I am in a relationship to God whereby I can hear His call.

There are strands of the call of God providentially at work that you know and no one else does. It is the threading of God's voice for you on some particular line, and it is no use to consult anyone else about it, or to say that other people are dull because they do not hear it. "I did not immediately confer with flesh and blood" (Gal. 1:16). You feel amazed at the sense of God's call, and in your eagerness you talk to someone else about it, and you find that they much prefer to talk about their breakfast. Then comes the danger that you are apt to become contemptuous. Keep that profound relationship between your soul and God.

The vision of the new life from God—"Most assuredly, I say to you, unless one is born again, he cannot see the kingdom of God" (John 3:3).

The power of the vision which the new birth gives refers to perception by the personal spirit, and the characteristic of being born from above is that you begin to discern the rule of God. God's rule was there all the time, but true to His nature; now you have received His nature, you can perceive His rule. It is a good thing to mark the times when you feel your personal spirit trembling on the verge of a new vision. It may be during a lecture or in prayer, you nearly see something, then it goes; don't be distressed. It is the evidence of the new life from God.

The life given by God is capable of immediately hearing the voice of God's own nature. Unless the nature of God comes into you, said Jesus to Nicodemus, you cannot understand Him; but if His nature comes into you, of course you will hear Him (John 3:3−8). Intuition is the power to sense things without reasoning, and is a better guide than what is stated explicitly; but there is something infinitely more satisfactory—the entrance of the Holy Spirit into a person at new birth enabling him or her to see the kingdom of God and to enter into it.

The vocation of the natural life for God—"But when it pleased God, who separated me from my mother's womb and called me through His grace, to reveal His Son in me, that I might preach Him among the Gentiles" (Gal. 1:15−16).

The call of God is the call according to the nature of God. Where we go in obedience to that call depends entirely on the providential circumstances which God engineers. The call of God is not a call to any particular service, although my interpretation of the call may be; the call to service is the echo of my identification with God. My contact with the nature of God has made me realize what I can do for God. Service is the outcome of what is fitted to my nature. God's call is fitted to His nature, and I never hear His call until I have received His nature. When I have received His nature, then His nature and mine work together; the Son of God reveals Himself in me, and I, in my natural life, serve the Son of God in ordinary ways, out of sheer downright devotion to Him.

The call to service is the result of my obedience to the realized call of God. Profoundly speaking, there is no call to service for God; it is my own actual "bit," the overflow of super abounding devotion to God. God does not have to come and tell me what I must do for Him; He brings me into a relationship with Himself where in I hear His call and understand what He wants me to do, and I do it out of sheer love to Him. To serve God is the deliberate love gift of a nature that has heard the call of God. When people say they have had a call to foreign service, or to any particular sphere of work, they mean that their relationship to God has enabled them to realize what they can do for God. Their natural fitting for service and the call of God is identified as one in them.

The vocation of the natural life for God is stated by Paul: "When it pleased God . . . to reveal His Son in me, that I might preach Him (sacramentally express Him) among the Gentiles" (Gal. 1:15-16).

The Call of God

To me . . . this grace was given, that I should preach among the Gentiles the unsearchable riches of Christ—Ephesians 3:8.

The consciousness of the call—Jer. 1:5; Amos 7:14–15.

We are apt to forget the mystic, supernatural touch of God which comes with His call. If a person can tell you how the call of God came and all about it, it is questionable whether he or she ever had the call. The call to be a professional may come in that explicit way, but the call of God is much more supernatural. The realization of the call of God may come as with a sudden thunderclap or by a gradual dawning, but in whatever way it comes, it comes with the undercurrent of the supernatural, almost the uncanny. It is always accompanied with a glow—something that cannot be put into words. We need to keep the atmosphere of our minds prepared by the Holy Spirit lest we forget the surprise of the touch of God on our lives.

"Before I formed you . . . I knew you" (Jer. 1:5). There are prenatal forces of God at work in our lives which we may be unconscious of for long enough; but at any moment there may break upon us the sudden consciousness of this incalculable, supernatural, surprising power that has hold of our lives before we have hold of them ourselves.

Another force at work is the prayers of other people. You are born into this world and will probably never know to whose prayers your life is the answer. It may be your own father and mother who have been used by God to dedicate your life to Him before you were born. The prayers may have remained apparently

17

unanswered, but in reality they are answered; and your life should be the answer in actuality. Our lives are the answers not only to the prayers of other people, but to the prayer the Holy Spirit is making for us, and to the prayers of our Lord Himself. When once you realize this, you will understand why it is that God does not say, "By your leave," when He comes into your life.

If we have been getting hard and metallic, untouched spiritually—not backsliding, but getting out of touch with God—we shall find the reason is that we are allowing things to come in between us and the sense of God's call. At any minute God may bring the wind of His Spirit across our lives, and we shall realize with startled minds that the work we have been doing in the meantime is so much rubbish (1 Cor. 3:12–13). There is so much self-chosen service. We say, "I think I will do this and that for God." Unless we work for God in accordance with His supernatural call, we shall meet havoc and disaster and upset. The moment the consciousness of the call of God dawns on us, we know it is not a choice of our own at all; the consciousness is of being held by a power we do not fully know. I chose you (John 15:16). If we are saved and sanctified, we are called to testify to it; but the call to preach is something infinitely other and belongs to a different category. Paul describes it as a necessity. "Woe is me, if I do not preach the gospel!" (1 Cor. 9:16).

"Then Amos answered . . . 'I was no prophet, neither was I a son of a prophet, but I was a sheepbreeder, and a tender of sycamore fruit. Then the Lord took me as I followed the flock, and the Lord said to me, "Go, prophesy to My people Israel' " (Amos 7:14–15). The only way I can begin to fulfill the call of God is by keeping my convictions out of the way, my convictions as to what I imagine I am fitted for. The fitting goes much deeper down than one's natural equipping.

Whenever the call of God is realized, there is the feeling, I am called to be a missionary. It is a universal feeling because "the love of God has been poured out in our hearts by the Holy Spirit" (Rom. 5:5), and "God so loved the world" (John 3:16). We make a blunder when we fix on the particular location for our service and say, "God called me there." When God shifts the location, the battle comes. Will I remain consistent to what I have said I am going to do, or be true to the insurgent call of God, and let Him locate me where He likes?

The most, seemingly, untoward circumstances will be used by God for the men and women He has called. How ever much of wrong or of the devil there may seem to be at work, if an individual is called of God, every force will be made to tell for God's purpose in the end. God watches all these things when once we agree with His purpose for us, and He will bring not only the conscious life, but all the deeper regions of life which we cannot reach, into harmony with His purpose. If the call of God is there, it is not within the power of untoward things to turn you. Your heart remains, not untouched by them, but unbroken, and you are surprised at yourself—Why didn't I go under here, and there? "I called you."

We try to make calls out of our own spiritual consecration, but when we are put right with God, He blights all our sentimental convictions and devotional calls. He brushes them all aside, and rivets us with a passion that is terrific to one thing we had never dreamed of, and in the condition of real communion with God, we overhear Him saying: "Whom shall I send, and who will go for Us?" And for one radiant, flashing moment we see what God wants, and say in conscious freedom, "Here am I! Send me."

The character of the call—1 Cor. 9:16.

Paul puts out of court the idea that the preaching of the gospel is chosen as the choice of a profession is made. He says it is a necessity laid upon him. He was called to preach, even from his mother's womb, although for years he did not recognize it.

Then suddenly the call awakened in him, and he realized that was what God had been after all the time.

There is no mention of sin in Paul's apprehension, that came after; it was an apprehension of the call of God, a call which "separated" him to the gospel. "He is a chosen vessel of Mine. . . . For I will show him how many things he must suffer for My name's sake" (Acts 9:15-16). God called him in order to use him as broken bread and poured out wine for others. When Paul realized God's call and knew the meaning of his life, there was no competitor for his strength. Is there anything competing for our strength in our devotion to the call of God? It is not the devil, but the "little foxes" that spoil the vines—the little annoyances, the little actual things that compete for our strength, and we are not able to pray; things come in between, and our hearts are troubled and our minds disturbed by them. We have forgotten what Jesus said, "As the Father has sent Me, I also send you" (John 20:21). Our Lord never allowed anything to disturb Him out of His oneness with the Father. Only one thing held Him, "Behold, I have come . . . to do Your will, O God" (Heb. 10:7). With us, there are things that compete for the strength that should be given to God only. Thank God for such places as Bible training colleges where God gives us time to be shut in quietly. He is letting us see how competitors for our strength will knock the consciousness of His call right out.

Have I been forgetting the character of God's call? Has there been a refusal to be made broken bread and poured out wine? If so, life is consequently is being lived on the threshold of conscious devotion and conscious declension. This always happens when I do not realize that it is God who engineers my circumstances, when I "despise the day of small things." I refuse to see God's hand in the circumstances of the weather that prevented me on such and such a day, I refuse to see God's hand in the routing of my life, and as a result there is no sense of arrestment by God, no being made broken bread and poured out wine for others, but a dryness and a deadness all through. Prayer has brought no light, studying God's word has brought no comfort. This has nothing to do with the soul's salvation, but with the obliteration of the character of God's call. Let me take a revision and see how, in the little things, God has not been first, but my notions, my affinities, consideration of my temperament.

If we are not in full, conscious allegiance to our Lord it has nothing to do with our personal salvation, but with this broken bread and poured out wine aspect of life. God can never make me wine if I object to the fingers He uses to crush me. If God would only crush me with His own fingers, and say, "Now, My son, I am going to make you broken bread and poured out wine in a particular way and everyone will know what I am doing." But when He uses someone who is not a Christian, or someone I particularly dislike, or some set of circumstances which I said I would never submit to, and begins to make these the crushers, I object.

I must never choose the scene of my own martyrdom, nor must I choose the things God will use in order to make me broken bread and poured out wine. His own Son did not choose. God chose for His Son that He should have a devil in His company for three years. We say, "I want angels; I want people better than myself; I want everything to be significantly from God, otherwise I cannot live the life, or do the thing properly; I always want to be gilt-edged." Let God do as He likes. If you are ever going to be wine to drink, you must be crushed. Grapes cannot be drunk; grapes are only wine when they have been crushed. I wonder what kind of coarse finger and thumb God has been using to squeeze you, and you have been like a marble and escaped? You are not ripe yet, and if God had squeezed you, the wine that came out would have been remarkably bitter. Let God go on with His crushing, because it will work His purpose in the end.

The commission of the call—John 20:21; Luke 4:18–19.

Have we answered God's call in every detail? Have we really been the "sent" ones of Jesus, as He was the sent One of God? We can soon know.

What has been competing for our strength? What kind of things have we objected to? What things have hindered our times of communion, so that we have had to pray about them when we had no business to be in the place where we could notice them? We ought to have been living in John 14:1, but our hearts have been troubled and we have taken account of the evil; consequently we have been less concerned about God's enterprises than about our own. Woe unto me, said Paul, if I do not keep concentrated on this one thing, that I am called of God for His service.

God puts us through discipline not for our own sakes, but for the sake of His purpose and His call. Never debate about anything God is putting you through, and never try to find out why you are going through it. Keep right with God and let Him do what He likes in your circumstances and you will find He is producing the kind of bread and wine that will be a benefit to others.

THE POINT OF SPIRITUAL HONOR

I am debtor both to Greeks, and to Barbarians—Romans 1:14.

Do I feel this sense of indebtedness to Christ that Paul felt with regard to every unsaved soul I meet, every unsaved nation? Is it a point of spiritual honor with me that I do not hoard blessings for myself? The point of spiritual honor in my life as a saint is the realization that I am a debtor to everyone on the face of the earth because of the redemption of the Lord Jesus Christ.

Paul realized that he owed everything to Jesus Christ, and it was in accordance with his sense of spiritual honor that he spent himself to the last ebb to express his indebtedness to Jesus Christ. When one is indwelt by the Holy Spirit, one never talks in cold logic, but in passionate inspiration. And the inspiration behind all Paul's utterances is the fact that he viewed Christ as his Creditor. For "I could wish that I myself were accursed from Christ for my brethren" (Rom. 9:3). The great characteristic of Paul's life was that he realized he was not his own; he had been bought with a price and he never forgot it. His whole life was based on that one thing. Paul sold himself to Christ—"the bondslave of Jesus." "For I determined not to know anything among you except Jesus Christ, and Him crucified" (1 Cor. 2:2).

We are apt to have the idea that a person called to the ministry is called to be a different kind of being from others. According to Jesus Christ, His minister is called to be the "doormat" of others, one who is their spiritual leader, but never their superior, "ourselves your bondservants for Jesus' sake" (2 Cor. 4:5). No matter how people treat me, Paul argues, they will never treat me with the hatred and spite with which I treated Jesus Christ; and as long as there is a human being who does not know Jesus Christ, I am a debtor to serve that person. When the realization comes home that Jesus Christ has served me to the end of all my meanness, my selfishness and sin, then nothing I meet with from others can exhaust my determination to serve them for His sake. I am not to come among people as their superior; I am to come among them as the love-slave of Jesus Christ, realizing that if I am worth anything at all, it is through redemption. That is the meaning of being made broken bread and poured out wine in reality.

"I have become all things to all men, that I might by all means save some" (1 Cor. 9:22). Paul attracted people to Jesus all the time, never to himself. He became a sacramental personality; that is, wherever he went Jesus Christ helped Himself to his life. (See 2 Cor 2:14.) Many of us are subtly serving our own ends, and Jesus Christ cannot help Himself to our lives; if I am abandoned to Jesus, I have no ends of my own to serve. Paul said, "I know how to be abased" (Phil. 4:12)—he knew how to be a doormat without resenting it, because the mainspring of his life was devotion to Jesus.

Thank God, when He has saves us He does give us something to do, some way of expressing our gratitude to Him. He gives us a great, noble sense of spiritual honor, the realization that we are debtors to everyone because of the redemption of Jesus Christ. The sense of our debt to Jesus is so overwhelming that we are passionately concerned for that brother, that friend, those unsaved nations; in relation to them we are the bondslaves of Jesus.

Am I doing anything to enable Jesus Christ to bring His redemption into actual manifestation in other lives? I can do it only if the Holy Spirit has wrought in me this sense of spiritual honor. When I realize what Jesus Christ has done for me, then I am a debtor to all human beings until they know Him too, not for their sakes, not because they will otherwise be lost, but because of Jesus Christ's redemption. Am I willing to sell myself to Jesus, to become simply His bondslave, in order that He may see "the labor of His soul and be satisfied" (Isa. 53:11)?

The great motive and inspiration of service is not that God has saved and sanctified me, or healed me. All that is a fact, but the great motive of service is the realization that every bit of my life that is of value I owe to His redemption; therefore I am a bondslave of Jesus. I realize with joy that I cannot live my own life; I am a debtor to Christ, and as such I can only realize the fulfillment of His purposes in my life. To realize this sense of spiritual honor means I am spoiled for this age, for this life, spoiled from every standpoint but this one, that I can disciple men and women to the Lord Jesus.

Paul was a lonely debtor in a world of repudiators. Does your friend repudiate the redemption of Jesus? Does the net result of your life work appeal to him or her only on one line, the line of redemption? Does he or she take no account of you on any other line? Never let anything deter you from spending for other souls every ounce of spiritual energy God gives you. There will be an actual manifestation of redemption in lives presently. Whatever you spend of yourself in the fulfilling of your sense of spiritual honor will come back to you in absolute re-creation, physical and moral and spiritual.

"If anyone sees his brother sinning a sin which does not lead to death, he will ask, and He will give him life for those who commit sin not leading to death" (1 John 5:16). Quit praying about yourself, and be spent in vicarious intercession as the bondslave of Jesus.

How many have we failed to bring through to God because of our crass unbelief in prayer? Jesus Christ places the emphasis on intercessory prayer—"He who believes in Me, the works that I do he will do also; and greater works than these he will do, because I go to My Father. And whatever you ask in My name, that I will do, that the Father may be glorified in the Son. If you ask anything in My name, I will do it" (John 14:12-14). That is reality; that is actuality! The actuality will take place—the almighty interaction of God in other lives in answer to prayer based on redemption, not to prayer based on human sympathy or human plaintiveness. When we pray on the basis of redemption, our prayers are made efficacious by the personal presence of the Holy Spirit who makes real in us what Jesus did for us. How God works in answer to prayer is a mystery that logic cannot penetrate, but that He does work in answer to prayer is gloriously true. We all have faith in God, but is our faith preeminent when it comes into contact with actualities? Our part in intercessory prayer is not to enter into the agony of intercession, but to utilize the commonsense circumstances God has placed us in, and the commonsense people He has put us among by His providence, to bring them before God's throne and collaborate with the Holy Spirit as He intercedes for them. That is how God is going to sweep the whole world with His saints.

Am I banking in unshaken faith on the redemption of Jesus Christ? Is it my conviction that everyone can be presented "perfect in Christ Jesus" (Col. 1:28)? Or do I allow people's sins and wrongs so to obliterate the power of redemption that I sink under them? Jesus said, "He who believes in Me . . . out of his heart will flow rivers of living water" (John 7:38); that is, by active belief in Jesus based on redemption, and by prayer and service based on that same redemption.

VISION, VALLEY, VERITY

Life is not as idle ore,
But iron dug from central gloom . . .
And batter'd by the shocks of doom
To shape and use.

It is always well to go back to the foundation truths revealed in God's Word regarding what He expects of the man or woman who wishes to be what He wants. "Called to be saints" (Rom. 1:7), that is what God expects.

Thank God for the sight of all you have never yet been. The vision is not an ecstasy or a dream, but a perfect understanding of what God wants. It is the divine light making manifest the calling of God. You may call the vision an emotion or a desire, but it is something that absorbs you. Learn to thank God for making known His demands. You have had the vision, but you are not there yet, by any means. You have not seen what God wants you to be but are not yet. Are you prepared to have this "iron dug from central gloom" battered into "shape and use"?

Battering conveys the idea of a blacksmith putting good metal into useful shape. The batterings of God come in commonplace days and commonplace ways; God is using the anvil to bring us into the shape of the vision. The length of time it takes God to do it depends on us. If we prefer to loll on the Mount of Transfiguration, to live on the memory of the vision, we are of no use to live with the ordinary stuff of which human life is made up. We do not have to live always in ecstasy and conscious contemplation of God, but to live in reliance on what we saw in the vision when we are in the midst of actualities. It is when we are going through the valley to prove whether we will be the choice ones that most of us turn tail. We are not prepared for the blows which must come if we are going to be turned into the shape of the vision. It does not matter with what the vision is connected, there is always something that corresponds to the valley of humiliation. God gives us the vision, then He takes us down to the valley to batter us into its shape, and it is in the valley that we faint and give way while all the time God is wanting to get us through to the reality.

Abraham—In Gen. **15**:1 we read, "After these things the word of the Lord came to Abram in a vision, saying, 'Do not be afraid, Abram. I am your shield, your exceedingly great reward.' " After the vision there followed the valley of humiliation, and Abram went through thirteen years of silence. Genesis 16 is an illustration of the danger of listening to good advice when it is dark instead of waiting for God to send the light. The act of Abram and Sarai produced a complexity in God's plan all down the ages. The intervening years brought Abram through his valley of humiliation. During those years of silence all his self-sufficiency was destroyed, every strand of self-reliance was broken; there was no possibility left of relying on commonsense ways, and when he had exhausted all human strength and wisdom, then God appeared to him. "When Abram was ninety-nine years old, the Lord appeared to Abram and said to him, 'I am Almighty God; walk before Me and be blameless' " (Gen. **17**:1). No vision this time, but reality. Abram, after his humiliation, was in a fit state to stand the reward—God Himself. Abraham became a man more sure of God than of anything else.

The one thing for which we are all being disciplined is to know that God is real. As soon as God becomes real, other people become shadows. Nothing other saints do or say can ever perturb the one who is built on the real God. "In all the world, my God, there is none but thee, there is none but thee."

The danger is to try to anticipate the actual fulfillment of the real vision. On the Mount of Transfiguration we saw clearly a vision of what God wanted, and we transacted business with God spiritually. Then immediately afterwards there was nothing but blank darkness. Remember Isaiah's word, "Who among you . . . walks in darkness and has no light? Let him trust in the name of the Lord and rely upon his God" (Isa. 50:10). The temptation is to work up enthusiasm, to kindle a fire of our own and walk in the light of it. God's "nothings" are His most positive answers. We have to stay on God and wait. Never try to help God to fulfill His Word.

Moses—"Now it came to pass in those days, when Moses was grown, that he went out to his brethren and looked at their burdens" (Exod. 2:11). That is an indication of the vision of God's purpose for Moses—the deliverance of his nation. It is a great moment in life when a person realizes that he or she has to go a solitary way. Moses was "learned in all the wisdom of the Egyptians" (Acts 7:22), a man in a royal setting by the providence of God, and he saw the burden of God's people and his whole heart and mind were ablaze with the vision that he was the one to deliver them. He was God's choice to deliver them. But not yet; there was something in the road, and God sent him into the wilderness to feed sheep for forty years. Imagine what those years must have meant to Moses, realizing on the threshold of his manhood the vision of what he was to do; seeing, as no one else could see, the burdens of his people and feeling in himself the certainty that he was the one to deliver them; how he would ponder over God's ways during those forty years.

Then we read that God appeared to Moses and said, "Come now, therefore, and I will send you to Pharaoh that you may bring My people, the children of Israel, out of Egypt" (Exod. 3:10). Forty years have passed since he had the vision, and there is a different characteristic in Moses now. It is no longer the big I am, but the little I am. When God comes with a renewal of the call, Moses has the quaver of the little I am—"Who am I that I should go?" (v. 11). The little I am always sulks when God says do. And the Almighty's reply to Moses is full of stirring indignation: "I AM WHO I AM. . . . Thus you shall say . . . 'I AM has sent me' " (v. 14). The big I am and the little I am have to go until there is no I am but God; He must dominate. Let the little I am be shriveled up in God's indignation. Is it not illuminating how God knows where we are, and the kennels we crawl into, no matter how much straw we hide under! He will show us up like a lightning flash. No human being knows human beings as God does.

"Here is a place by Me, and you shall stand on the rock" (Exod. 33:21). Moses has come to the reality of all realities, recognition by God. The place in God's mind for Moses is by Him on the rock, recognized by God as His true yokefellow. Nothing can deflect the life that has once been placed by God on the rock. After the forty years of humiliation Moses is in a fit state to receive the recognition of God without being unduly lifted up.

"Here is a place by Me." None ever get beside God who have not first been beside themselves and knocked out of their wits with worry and anxiety about the mess they have made of things. That is the meaning of conviction of sin, the realization, "What a fool I have been! How wicked and vile! And I ought to have been this and that!"

Moses' experience was of the type in which the certainty is brought home that God has been preparing you for something, and you realize that you potentially have the power to do what He wants. You can recall the perfect reality of the vision, the clear understanding of what God said to you then. You say, "I know He said it, I almost saw Him, it was so real. I know God called me to be a missionary. But it was a long time ago, and I suppose I was mistaken, for look at me now, something in an office." You know you were not mistaken. The call was right, but you were not ready for it. God has to season us. There has to be a time of humiliation before the vision is turned into verity. We have to learn not only how useless we are, but how marvelously mighty God is. "Many are called" (Matt. 20:16), but few prove the choice ones.

Think of the enormous leisure of God! He never is in a hurry. We are in such a frantic hurry. We get down before God and pray, then we get up and say, "It is all done now," and in the light of the glory of the vision we go forth to do the thing. But it is not real, and God has to take us into the valley and put us through fires and floods to batter us into shape, until we get into the condition in which He can trust us with the reality of His recognition of us.

Isaiah—"In the year that King Uzziah died, I saw the Lord sitting on a throne, high and lifted up, and the train of His robe filled the temple" (Isa. 6:1).

Isaiah's vision stands for another type of the call of God. In the profound grief of the greatest bereavement of his life Isaiah saw the Lord, and right on top of the vision came deep and profound dejection on account of his sin and unworthiness. "Woe is me, for I am undone! Because I am a man of unclean lips, and I dwell in the midst of a people of unclean lips; for my eyes have seen the King, the Lord of hosts" (v. 5). The effect of the vision of the holiness of the Lord was to bring home to Isaiah that he was a man of unclean lips; there was deep dejection at his utter unfitness to be anything like what he had seen. Then the live coal from off the altar was laid on his mouth—the cleansing fire was applied where the sin had been concentrated—and in the communion with God resulting from his intense spiritual cleansing, Isaiah overheard God say, "Whom shall I send, and who will go for Us?" (v. 8). And from heartbreak and disenchantment to simple, humble attachment, he said, "Here am I! Send me." Isaiah was made the representative of God.

Each one of us has a counterpart somewhere in the experiences of these three men of God. In the case of Abraham, the valley of humiliation lasted thirteen years; of Moses, forty years; of Isaiah, a few minutes. No two of us are alike; each one stands alone before God. Your valley may be a darkness where you have nothing but your duty to guide you, no voice, no thrill, but just steady, plodding duty. Or it may be a deep, agonizing dejection at the realization of your unfitness and uncleanness and insufficiency. Let God put you on His wheel and whirl you as He likes, and as sure as God is God and you are you, you will turn out exactly in accordance with the vision He gave you. Don't lose heart in the process.

If ever we had the vision, and all of us probably have had—it may have been when we were little children, or when we were very ill, or after a bereavement—we may try as we like to be satisfied on a lower level, but God will not let us. The goads of God are in, and it is hard to kick against them. Ever since we first had the vision God has been at work getting us through the valley of humiliation, battering us into the shape of the vision. Over and over again we have tried to get out of God's hands and batter ourselves into our own shape, "Now this is the place I must be; this is what the vision means." Keep paying the price. Let God see that you are willing to live up to the vision.

Our Lord's Surprise Visits

Let your waist be girded and your lamps burning; and
you yourselves be like men who wait for their master
. . . for the Son of Man is coming at an hour you do
not expect—Luke 12:35–36, 40.

The greatest need of the missionary is to be ready to face
Jesus Christ at any and every turn, and it is not easy to be ready
to do that, whatever our experience of sanctification may be. The
great battle all along is not so much against sin as against being so
absorbed in work that we are not ready to face Jesus Christ. The
one great need is not to face our beliefs and our creeds, or the
question of whether we are of any use or not, but to face our
Lord. This attitude of being ready to face Him means more and
more disentanglement from so-called religious work, and more
and more intense spiritual reality in so-called secular work. The
whole meaning of the Christian life from our Lord's standpoint is
to be ready for Him.

The element of surprise is always the note of the life of the
Holy Spirit in us. We are born again by the great surprise—"The
wind blows where it wishes, and you hear the sound of it, but
cannot tell where it comes from, and where it goes. So is every
one who is born of the Spirit" (John 3:8). Human beings cannot
tie up the wind, it blows where it will; neither can the work of
the Holy Spirit be tied up in logical methods. Jesus never comes
where we expect Him. If He did He would not have said,
"Watch. . . . also be ready, for the Son of Man is coming at an
hour you do not expect" (Matt. 24:42, 44). Jesus appears in the
most illogical connections, where we least expect Him, and the

only way a worker can keep true to God amidst the difficulties of work either in this country or in other lands is to be ready for His surprise visits.

We do not have to depend on the prayers of other people, nor to look for the sympathy of God's children, but to be ready for the Lord. It is this intense reality of expecting Him at every turn that gives life the attitude of child wonder that Jesus wants it to have. When we are rightly related to God, life is full of spontaneous, joyful uncertainty, and expectancy. We do not know what God is going to do next and He packs our lives with surprises all the time.

That is the line on which our Lord always comes, and the line on which we are not apt to look for Him. It comes home in ways like this: You have prepared a sermon or an address very carefully and feel that God gave you a good time in the delivery of it, but nothing happens. At another time you talk without much consideration, and suddenly there comes the certainty, "Why, that is the Lord! That was said by Him, not by me."

Beware of the idea that we can tie up the Lord Jesus by spiritual logic: "This is where He will come, and that is where He will not come." If we are going to be ready for Jesus whenever He comes, we must stop being religious—using religion as a kind of higher culture—and become spiritually real, alert and ready for Him.

"Let your waist be girded." It is impossible to run in the loose Eastern garments unless they are girded up. The writer to the Hebrews counsels us to "lay aside every weight, and the sin which so easily ensnares us" (Heb. 12:1). He is not speaking of inbred sin, but of the spirit of the religious age in which we live which will entangle the feet of the saints and hinder our running the race. Loose, trailing, uninspired thinking about sin will very soon trip us up. Gird up your thinking about sin, about holiness, about the eternal realities, and about the call of the unseen things.

It is amazing to see the unreadiness of even some of the most spiritual people. They are continually clogged and tripped up by the wrong things. If we are looking to Jesus and avoiding the spirit of the religious age in which we live, and setting our hearts on thinking along Jesus Christ's lines, we shall be called impractical and dreamy; but when He appears in the burden and the heat of the day only we shall be ready. When you meet a man or woman who puts Jesus Christ first, knit that one to your soul.

"And your lamps burning; and you yourselves be like men who wait for their master." Am I looking for my Lord where no one sees me but God? In my study, am I a wool-gatherer or like one looking for my Lord? Am I looking for the Lord in my home, in my contact with other people—is the lamp of conscience trimmed and burning there? Our Lord does not trim the lamp, we have to, and it is not done once for all, but once and for always, that is, always now. Conscience in a saint will make you look after your scruples according to the light of God. As servants of God in other lands you will have to go among people whose lives are twisted and perverted by unconscious corruption, but if your conscience is as a lamp trimmed and burning, then the Lord can visit others through you at any second.

Is the lamp of your affections burning clear? If not, you will lose out in that way quicker than in any other. Inordinate affection means that you have allowed convictions to go to the winds. Keep the center of your heart for Jesus Christ and watch inordinate affection as you would the devil. There is more reason to be found there as to why Christians are not ready for Jesus Christ's surprise visits than anywhere else.

Is the lamp of hope burning bright? "And everyone who has this hope in Him purifies himself" (1 John 3:3). And what a hope it is! "We shall see Him as He is" (1 John 3:2). "Blessed are those servants whom the master, when he comes, will find watching" (Luke 12:37).

Do you imagine that there will be crowds to come up to that standard? Jesus said no, it is one here and one there, always "a little flock." Our Lord is not talking of salvation, but about being His servants. Whenever Jesus got down to His truth, the crowds left Him. (See John 6:66.) Today the craze is for crowds.

The one great need for the missionary is to be ready for Jesus Christ, and we cannot be ready unless we have seen Him. We must trust no one, not the finest saint who ever walked this earth, if once he hinders our sight of Jesus. It is Jesus Christ we have to be ready to meet; Jesus Christ for whom we must work.

Readiness implies a right relationship to God and a knowledge of where we are at present. We are so busy telling God where we would like to go. Most of us are waiting for some great opportunity—something that is sensational—then we cry, "Here am I! Send me." Whenever Jesus is in the ascendant, in revival times, when the exciting moment comes, we are there; but readiness for God and for His work means that we are ready to do the tiniest thing or the great big thing, it makes no difference. We are so built that we must have sympathy or we will never do our best. But this instinct is apt to be prostituted unless we get burned into our hearts an understanding of what Jesus said: "Lo, I am with you always" (Matt. 28:20). He is the One who is surrounding us, listening and sympathizing and encouraging. Our audience is God, not God's people, but God Himself. The saint who realizes this can never be discouraged no matter where he or she goes.

The audience of a ready saint is God. He is the arena of all our actions. To know that God is the One who sympathizes and understands and watches us will bring the ready soul into touch and sympathy with God. What we lack today is sympathy with God's point of view. When once we get into sympathy with God, He will bring us into touch with His purposes and with the real needs of men and women.

"You shall be witnesses to Me" (Acts 1:8). To witness to Jesus means that when any duty presents itself we hear His voice just as He heard His Father's voice, and we are ready for it with all the alertness of our love for Him. The knowledge that Jesus expects to do with us as His Father did with Him becomes the closely imbedded conception of our lives: "one as We are" (John 17:11). That is the only simplicity there is, the simplicity of a heart relationship to Jesus.

Beware of believing that the human soul is simple, or that human life is simple. Our relationship to God in Christ is the only simple thing there is. If the devil succeeds in making this relationship complicated, then the human soul and human life will appear to be simple, whereas in reality they are far too complex for us to touch. That is why Paul said, "I fear, lest . . . your minds may be corrupted from the simplicity that is in Christ" (2 Cor. 11:3). We have to keep that pristine simplicity free from anything like tarnish.

Be ready for the sudden, surprise visits of our Lord. Remember there is no such thing as prominent service and obscure service; it is all the same with God, and God knows better than we ourselves what we are ready to do. Think of the time we waste trying to get ready when God gives the call! A ready person never needs to get ready. The bush that burned with fire and was not consumed is the symbol for everything that surrounds the ready saint. Anyone can see an ordinary bush—the ready soul sees it ablaze with God.

The Go of Preparation

Matthew 5:23–24

> Nerve us with patience, Lord, to toil or rest,
>   Toiling at rest on our allotted level,
> Unsnared, unscared by world or flesh or devil,
> Fulfilling the good will of Thy behest.
>   Not careful here to hoard, not here to revel,
> But waiting for our treasure and our zest
> Beyond the facing splendor of the west,
>   Beyond this deathstruck life and deadlier evil.
> Not with the sparrow building here a house,
>   But with the swallow tabernacling, so
>   As still to poise alert, to rise and go
> On eagle wings, with wing outspeeding wills,
> Beyond earth's gourds and past her almond boughs—
>   Past utmost bound of the everlasting hills.

Preparation is not something suddenly accomplished but a process steadily maintained. It is easy to imagine that we get to a settled state of experience where we are complete and ready. But in work for God it is always preparation and preparation. Moral preparation comes before intellectual preparation, because moral integrity is of more practical value than any amount of mental insight.

Moral Preparation

In writing to the Philippians Paul mentions two perfections: "not that I . . . am already perfected" (3:12); "Therefore let us, as many as are mature (perfect, KJV) . . ." (3:15).

38

The first refers to the perfection of attainment; the second to the perfection of adjustment to God. When by the experience of sanctification we are in perfect adjustment to God, we can begin to live the perfect life, that is, we can begin to attain.

A child is a perfect human being, so is an adult; what is the difference? The one is not yet grown, the other is full grown. When we are sanctified, we are perfectly adjusted to God but we have done nothing yet, we are simply perfectly fit to begin. The whole life is right, undeserving of censure in the sight of God; now we can begin to attain in our bodily life, to prove that we are perfectly adjusted.

We are in the quarry now and God is hewing us out. God's Spirit gathers and marks the stones, then they have to be blasted out of their holdings by the dynamite of the Holy Spirit to be chiseled and shaped, and then lifted into the heavenly places. God grant that many may go through the quarrying and the chiseling and the placing. Think of the scrutiny of Jesus Christ that each one of us has to face! Think of His eyes fastening on us and pointing us out before God as He says, "Father, that is My work; that is the meaning of Gethsemane, that is the meaning of Calvary. I did all that man's work in him, all that woman's work in her; now You can use them."

Heroism and sacrifice—"Therefore if you bring your gift to the altar . . ." (Matt. 5: 23). The Jews were scrupulous over external purity. If, on the way to the temple to offer his Passover lamb, a man would recollect that he had leaven in his house, he had to hasten back and remove the leaven; and then when he had purged his house, carry his offering to the altar.

The sense of the heroic appeals readily to a young Christian. Take Peter, for instance. Humanly speaking Peter was attracted to Jesus by his sense of the heroic. When Jesus said, "Follow Me" (Matt. 4:19), Peter followed at once; it was no cross to him. It would have been a bigger cross not to follow, for the spell of Jesus Christ was on him. We are apt to underestimate this enthusiastic sense of the heroic. It would be a terrible thing to be incapable of it, a terrible thing to be incapable of making such a declaration as Peter made: "I will lay down my life for Your sake" (John 13:37). Peter meant what he said, but he did not know himself.

The scrutiny of our Lord's words brings the tide of enthusiasm suddenly to the test. Many of us have come to the altar for service, but are we willing to bind the sacrifice with cords to the horns of the altar? The altar means fire—burning and purification and insulation—for one purpose: to detach us to God. Along with the sense of the heroic there is a base element of selfishness, a lurking desire to fix the scene of our own martyrdom. We feel if only we could fix the place and the spectators, we could go all lengths. But God fixes the place.

The illustration our Lord used in Matt. 5:21–22 is unfamiliar to us, but the application is familiar. He was illustrating the descending scale of wrong tempers of mind. An angry person was in danger of being brought before the rulers for judgment; a contemptuous, disdainful one was regarded in the same way as a blasphemer and was brought before the ruler of the Sanhedrin; one who gave way to abuse was in danger of being classed with criminals and flung out on the scrap heaps where the fires burned up the rubbish.

Hardship and sensitivity—"And there remember that your brother has something against you . . ."

Not—there you rake up a morbid sensitivity, but—there you remember. The inference is that it is brought to your conscious mind by the Spirit of God. Never object to the intense sensitivity of the Holy Spirit in you when He is educating you down to the scruple. When we are first put right with God, it is the great general principles that are at work, then God begins to make the conscience sensitive. Don't quench the Spirit. His checks are so tiny that common sense cannot detect them. If there is a sense of being out of touch with God, it is at the peril of your soul you go and ask someone else what you have done wrong. You must go direct to God. The other soul is never so keen as the Spirit of God. When He checks, never debate but obey at once.

It is not a question of having had the law of God put in front of your mind, "This is what you must do and that is what you must not do," and then deliberate disobedience on your part. It is more an instinct of the spirit, an instantaneous feeling, a still, small voice which we can easily quench. But if we do quench it we become soiled, and every time the check comes and we do not heed it the soiling is deepened. "Do not grieve the Holy Spirit" (Eph. 4:30). He does not come with a voice like thunder, with strong emphatic utterance. That may come ultimately, but at the beginning His voice is as gentle as a breath. At the same time it carries an imperative compulsion: we know the voice must be obeyed.

The go of preparation is to let the Word of God scrutinize. We are full of the sense of heroic sacrifice, and it seems hard to be reminded of things that happened in the past; but the thing that the Holy Spirit is detecting is that disposition in us that will never work in His service.

Over and over again people have gone into work for God in order to evade concentration on God on these lines. The note of false enthusiasm is the condition of the unbelieving. The need is made the call; but it is an artificial enthusiasm. No enthusiasm for humanity will ever stand the strain that Jesus Christ will put on His workers. Only one thing will stand the strain and that is the personal relationship to Jesus of a man or woman who has gone through the mill of God's spring cleaning until there is one purpose only: "I am here for God to use me as He wills."

Mental Preparation

Direction by first impulse—"Leave your gift there before the altar . . ." (Matt. 5:24).

When God shows you there is something to do, don't be sulky with God. Don't say, "Oh well, I suppose after all God does not want me." Don't affect a heaviness of soul because other missionaries are not what they ought to be; don't criticize the missionary society you belong to. Our Lord's instruction is that you leave your gift and go; take your direction from the conviction He gave you when you first offered yourself to Him. Have nothing to hide from God. If you have, then let God riddle you with His light. If there is sin, confess it, not admit it. Are you willing to obey your Lord and Master in this particular, no matter what the humiliation may be to your right to yourself?

Departure to the former condition—". . . and go your way."

Our Lord's direction is simple—go back the way you came, and put that thing right. Never put a thing aside because it is insignificant. If you trace it down, the insignificant thing has at the back of it the disposition of your right to yourself. Trace a scruple to its base and you find a pyramid; if you deal with a scruple, God will deal with the pyramid. The thing itself may be a detail; it is the disposition behind that is wrong, the refusal to give up your right to yourself—the thing God intends us to do if we are ever going to be disciples.

Never discard a conviction; if it is important enough for the Spirit of God to have brought it to your mind, that is the thing He is detecting. You were looking for a great big thing to do, and God is telling you of some tiny thing; but at the back of the tiny thing is the central citadel of obstinacy. "Do you think I am going to humiliate myself? Besides, if I do this thing, it will cause others to stumble." No one will ever stumble because of us if we do what is right and obey what God indicates. Never remain true to a former confession of faith when God's Spirit indicates there is something else for you to do. Go the way indicated by the conviction given you at the altar. It is marvelous what God detects in us for His spring cleaning!

Spiritual Preparation

The unblameable attitude in human life—"First be reconciled to your brother . . ."

Unblameable does not mean faultless, but undeserving of censure. Jesus is saying, "Have an attitude of mind and temper of spirit to the one who has something against you that makes reconciliation as natural and as easy as breathing." Jesus does not mention the other person. He says you go. There is no question of rights. The stamp of the saint is that you can waive your own rights and obey the Lord Jesus. That is the temper of soul to be in all through, unblameable in your attitude towards one another. Our Lord demands that there not be a trace of resentment, even suppressed. A wrong temper of mind is the most blameworthy thing there is. It is not only what we say but what we think that tells.

The unblameable attitude in divine life—". . . and then come and offer your gift."

The process is clearly marked by our Lord: first, the heroic spirit of sacrifice, then the sudden checking by the sensitivity of the Holy Spirit; the stopping at the point of conviction, and the going in obedience to God's word; constructing an unblameable attitude of mind and temper to the one with whom we were wrong; and then the glad, simple, unhindered offering of our gift to God.

The Go of Renunciation

Luke 9:57–62

Braver souls for truth may bleed;
Ask us not of noble deed!
Small our share in Christ's redemption—
From His war we claim exemption.
Not for us the cup was drained;
Not for us the cross of thorn
On His bleeding brow was borne:
Not for us the spear was stained
With the blood from out His side,
Not for us the Crucified.
Let His hands and feet be torn!
On the list we come but low:
Nor for us the cross was taken,
Us no bugle call can waken
To the combat, soldier fashion.

Missionary enterprise, to be Christian, must be based on the passion of obedience, not on the pathos of pity. The thing that moves us today is pity for the multitude; the thing that makes a missionary is the sight of what Jesus did on the Cross, and to have heard Him say Go. Jesus Christ pays no attention whatever to our sentiment. In the New Testament the emphasis is not on the needs of mankind, but on the command of Christ, Go. The only safeguard in Christian work is to go steadily back to first principles.

The Rigor of Rejection

The declaration of dignified devotion—"Then a certain scribe came (RSV marg. "one scribe," implying a scribe of the ruling class.) and said to Him, 'Teacher, I will follow You wherever You go' " (Matt. 8:19).

Any remnant of consciousness that position in society or profession is of value to Jesus is rigorously rejected by our Lord. The first thing we think of is just that very thing. "If that person were saved, what a wonderful influence such a one would be for Jesus Christ." Any sense that the cause of Christ will be benefited if I give myself to it or any trace of listening to the suggestion of others that I should be of value in my Lord's service receives no encouragement from Jesus. The ruggedness of our Lord's presentation of things strikes us as being very harsh. All He said to this scribe was, "Foxes have holes and birds of the air have nests, but the Son of Man has nowhere to lay His head" (Matt. 8:20). Our Lord is no respecter of persons. We would have treated this man very differently—"Fancy losing the opportunity of that man! Fancy bringing a north wind about him that froze him and turned him away discouraged."

We do respect persons; we do place confidence in the flesh. We need to go back to the center of the Christian faith, the Cross of Jesus Christ. It is not a question of education or of personal qualifications, but of understanding who Jesus is, and knowing what He has done for us.

What is the test we put first for work at home or abroad? Sentimentally, we put the call of God first, but actually we are inclined to fix on the abilities of certain people. Our Lord pays not the remotest attention to natural abilities or natural virtues. He heeds only one thing—"Does that individual discern who I am? Does that one know the meaning of My Cross?" The men and women Jesus Christ is going to use in His enterprises are those in whom He has done everything. Our Lord lays down the conditions of discipleship in Luke 14:26–27, 33, and implies that the only people He will use in His building enterprises are those who love Him personally, passionately, and devotedly, beyond any of the closest relationships on earth.

The detection of discernment—"But Jesus did not commit Himself to them, because He knew all men . . . for He knew what was in man" (John 2:24–25).

Always take these words of Jesus into account in interpreting His replies and you will learn never to apologize for your Lord. Our Lord's attitude to this particular scribe was one of severe discouragement, because He knew what was in him. Jesus Christ's answers are never based on caprice, but on a knowledge of what is in people. The answers of Jesus hurt and offend until there is nothing left to hurt or offend (see Matt. 11:6).

If we have never been hurt by a statement of Jesus it is questionable whether we have ever really heard Him speak. Jesus Christ has no tenderness whatever towards anything that is ultimately going to ruin a person for the service of God. If the Spirit of God brings to mind a word of the Lord that hurts, we may be perfectly certain there is something He wants to hurt to death.

The rigor of rejection leaves nothing but my Lord and myself and a forlorn hope. "Let the hundreds come or go," says Jesus, "your guiding star must be your relationship to Me, and I have nowhere to lay My head."

The discouragement of drastic discipline—"You do not know what you ask. Are you able to drink the cup that I am about to drink?" (Matt. 20:22).

The words of Jesus to the scribe knock the heart out of self-consciousness in service for Jesus—serving Jesus because it pleases one's self. Jesus told him that if he followed Him he would be homeless and possessionless. Do you expect to be a successful worker for Jesus if you are a disciple of His? Then you are doomed to a discouraging disappointment. Our Lord never called us to successful service. He calls us to present Him. "I, if I am lifted up from the earth, will draw all peoples to myself" (John 12:32). God saves; we are sent out to present Jesus Christ and His Cross, and to disciple the souls He saves. The reason we do not make disciples is that we are not disciples ourselves; we are out for our own ends.

The Rally of Reluctance

Luke 9:59–60

The solicitation of the Lord—"Then He said to another, 'Follow me' " (v.59).

Jesus said "Follow Me" to a man who was immediately awakened into a ferment of sensitive apprehension. When the call of God begins to dawn, we are full of "why," and "but," and "what will happen if I do?" This man did not want to disappoint Jesus, nor to hurt his father. When Jesus called him, he was staggered into sensitive apprehension.

The sensitivity of the loyal—"Lord, let me first to go and bury my father."

When Jesus calls, there is the ordeal of conflicting loyalties. Probably the most intense discipline we have to go through is that of learning loyalty to God by the path of what looks like disloyalty to our friends. This is stated in its profoundest form in Luke 14:26, "If anyone comes to Me and does not hate his own father and mother, wife and children, brothers and sisters, yes, and his own life also, he cannot be My disciple."

Learn to estimate the disproportion in your loyalties. Some will put the Lord to open shame before being disloyal to friends. But when you learn how to lay down your life for your Friend

Jesus Christ other people promptly become shadows until they become realities in Him. When a sense of loyalty to father or mother perplexes you, picture Jesus showing you His pierced hands and feet and wounded side and thorn-crowned head, and hear Him say, "Think what that must have meant to My mother, and it is I who call you to follow Me."

No one could have had a more sensitive love in human relationship than Jesus; yet He said there are times when love to father and mother must be hatred in comparison to our love for Him. The sense of loyalty to father or mother or friends may easily slander Jesus because it implies that He does not understand our duties to them. If Jesus had been loyal to His earthly mother He would have been a traitor to His Father's purpose. Obedience to the call of Christ nearly always costs everything to two people—the one who is called, and the one who loves that one. We put sensitive loyalty to relationships in place of loyalty to Jesus; every other love is put first and He has to take the last place. We will readily give up sin and worldliness, but God calls us to give up the very closest, noblest, and most right tie we have, if it enters into competition with His call. Beware of the inclination to dictate to God as to what you will allow to happen if you obey Him.

The strenuousness of the leaving—"Jesus said to him, 'Let the dead bury their own dead, but you go and preach the kingdom of God' " (v. 16).

These words sound stern, but it must be remembered that Jesus spoke them to only one class, to those who realized duty to a parent. There are only too many who are willing to leave father and mother to preach the gospel in other lands. Always keep our Lord's sayings in their setting, and before taking a word of Jesus for yourself, see that yours is a similar case. In a conflict of loyalties, obey Jesus at all costs, and you will find that He will remember your parents, as He, on the cross, remembered His own mother.

The Renunciation of Reservations

Luke 9:61-62

The blind devotion of the first enthusiasm has to be pulled down into discipline.

The volunteer of enthusiasm—"Another . . . said, 'Lord, I will follow You, but . . .'" (v. 61).

The one who says "Yes, Lord, but," is always the one who is fiercely ready, but never goes. This man had one or two reservations, and one of them was that he wanted a valedictory service.

The vacillation of endearments—". . . let me first go and bid them farewell who are at my house."

Beware of the vacillation that comes through thinking of the Marys and Johns I love at home, my little mission, my church, my native place; it is apt to develop into wanting to fix the scene of my own martyrdom. The exacting call of Jesus leaves no margins of good-byes, because good-bye, as it is often used, is pagan, not Christian.

The voice of exactitude—"No one, having put his hand to the plow, and looking back, is fit for the kingdom of God" (v. 62).

In order to plow a straight furrow you must look neither at the plow nor behind you, but at the far end of the field ahead. When the call of God comes, begin to go and never stop going no matter how many delightful resting places there may be on the way.

Christ's call is "Follow Me." Our attitude ought to be, "Lord, if it is You, command me come to You" (Matt. 14:28), and Jesus will say Come.

The Go of Unconditional Identification

Mark 10:17–24, Matthew 19:16–22

> Then came a slow
> And strangling failure . . . .
> Yet felt somehow
> A mighty power was brooding, taking shape
> Within me; and this lasted till one night
> When, as I sat revolving it and more,
> A still small voice from without said,—Seest thou not,
> Desponding child, where spring defeat and loss?
> Even from thy strength . . . .
> Know, not for knowing's sake,
> But to become a star to men for ever;
> Know, for the gain it gets, the praise it brings,
> The wonder it inspires, the love it breeds:
> Look one step onward, and secure that step!

When the rich young ruler saw Jesus he wanted to be like Him; he had the master passion to be perfect. Anything less than the desire to be perfect in a profession or calling is humbug, and so in religion. Beware of quibbling over the word "perfection." It does not refer to the full consummation of one's powers, it simply means perfect fitness for doing the will of God; a perfect adjustment to God until all the powers are perfectly fitted to do His will.

The Look and the Loving of the Lord

"Then Jesus, looking at him . . ." (Mark 10:21).

Who is the Lord? This question must be answered by everyone—who is ruling me? In our Lord's calling of a disciple He never puts personal holiness in the front; He puts in the front absolute annihilation of my right to myself and unconditional identification with Himself—such a relationship with Him that there is no other relationship on earth in comparison. Luke 14:26 has nothing to do with salvation and sanctification, it has to do with unconditional identification with Jesus. None of us know the absolute go of abandon to Jesus until we are in unconditional identification with Him.

Have you ever realized who the Lord is in your life? The call to service is not the outcome of an experience of salvation and sanctification; there must be the recognition of Jesus Christ as Lord and Master as well as Savior. "Who do you say that I am?" (Matt. 16:15). That is the abiding test. Jesus Christ makes human destiny depend absolutely on who humans say He is. Membership of His Church is based on that one thing only, a recognition of who Jesus is and the public confession of it. Anyone who knows who Jesus is has had that revelation from God. "Blessed are you, Simon Bar-jonah, for flesh and blood has not revealed this to you, but My Father who is in heaven. And I also say to you that you are Peter, and on this rock I will build My church" (Matt. 16:17−18). What rock? The rock of the knowledge of who Jesus is and the confession of it.

"Now behold, one came and said to Him, 'Good Teacher, what good thing shall I do that I may have eternal life?' So He said to him, 'Why do you call Me good? No one is good but One, that is God' " (Matt. 19:16−17). "If I am only a good man, it is of no more use to come to Me than to anyone else; but if your coming means that you discern who I am," then comes the first condition: "If you want to enter into life, keep the commandments." The rich young ruler had to realize that there is only One who is good—God; and the only "good thing" from

Jesus Christ's point of view is union with that One, with nothing in between, and the steady maintenance of that union.

What is His look? "Then Jesus, looking at him, loved him" (Mark 10:21).

When Jesus saw the sterling worth and uprightness of the rich young ruler, He loved him. Natural virtues are lovely in the sight of Jesus because He sees in them His Father's former handiwork.

Has Jesus ever looked at you? Get rid of your experiences as you ask yourself that question. Experiences may be a barrier to our knowing Jesus; we forget Him in being taken up with what He has done for us. The look of Jesus transforms and transfigures. His look means the heart broken for ever from allegiance to any but Himself. Where you are "soft" with God is where the Lord has looked upon you; where you are hard and vindictive, insistent on your own way, certain that other people are more likely to be wrong than you, is where whole tracts of your nature have never been transformed by His gaze.

What is His love? The love of Jesus spoils us for every other interest in life except discipling men and women to Him. It is woe to every other ambition when once Christ fixes His love on a man or woman consciously. The love Jesus fixed on this man resulted in the biggest sorrow he ever had, "But he was sad . . . and went away sorrowful" (Mark 10:22).

The Lack and Longing of the Loved

What do I still lack—Our Lord instantly presses another penetrating if: "If you want to be perfect" (Matt. 19:21). Entrance into life is the recognition of who Jesus is, and we only recognize Him by the power of the Holy Spirit. Unless this recognition of Jesus is put first, we shall present a lame type of Christianity that excludes the type of individual represented by this young ruler. In the majority of cases recognition of who Jesus is comes before conviction of sin. This second if is far more searching—"If you want to be perfect"—then come the conditions.

Do I really want to be perfect? Do I really desire at all cost to every other interest that God should make me perfect? Can I say with Murray McCheyne, "Lord, make me as holy as You can make a saved sinner." Is that really the desire of my heart? When we are right with God, He gives us our desires and aspirations. Our Lord had only one desire, and that was to do the will of His Father, and to have this desire is the characteristic of a disciple. One thing you lack—"Go . . . sell whatever you have and give to the poor . . . and come . . . follow Me" (Mark 10:21).

These words mean a voluntary abandoning of riches and a deliberate, devoted attachment to Jesus Christ. We are so desperately wise in our own conceit that we continually behave as if Jesus did not mean what He said, and we spiritualize meaning into thin air. Jesus saw that this man depended on his riches. If He came to you or to me He might not say that, but He would say something that dealt with whatever He saw we were depending on. "Sell whatever you have," strip yourself of every possession, disengage yourself from all things until you are a naked soul; be a person merely and then give your humanity to God. Reduce yourself until nothing remains but your consciousness of yourself, and then cast that consciousness at the feet of Jesus Christ.

One right thing to do—Our Lord is not talking about salvation, but if you want to be perfect, those are the conditions; you need not accept them unless you like. You are at perfect liberty to say, "No, thank you, I am much obliged for being delivered from hell and the abominations of sin, but this is just too much to expect. I have my own interests in life." Sell all you have, said Jesus, barter it, obliterate it.

Never push an experience you have had into a principle by which to guide others. If you take what Jesus said to this man and make it mean that He taught we were to own nothing, you are evading what He taught by making it external. Our Lord told the rich young ruler to loosen himself from his property because that was the thing that was holding him. The principle is one of fundamental death to possessions while being careful to use them aright.

Am I prepared to strip myself of what I possess in property, in virtues, in the estimation of others—to count all things to be loss—in order to win Christ? I can be so rich in poverty, so rich in the consciousness that I am nobody, that I shall never be a disciple; and I can be so rich in the consciousness that I am somebody that I shall never be a disciple. Am I willing to be destitute even of the sense that I am destitute? It is not a question of giving up outside things but of making myself destitute to myself, reducing myself to a mere consciousness, and giving that to Jesus Christ. I must reduce myself until I am a mere conscious human being, I must fundamentally renounce possessions of all kinds (not to save my soul—only one thing saves a soul: absolute reliance on the Lord Jesus) and then give that human being to Jesus.

"Go your way, sell." Jesus did not say sell all you have and give the proceeds to the deserving poor; nor did He say consecrate all you have to My service. Jesus Christ does not claim any of our possessions. One of the most subtle errors is that God wants our possessions. He does not; they are not of any use to Him. He does not want my property, He wants my self. "Sell whatever you have and give the proceeds away; but as for you—you come and follow Me."

The Light and Leading of the Life

"And you will have treasure in heaven; and come, follow Me" (Matt. 19:21).

The reduction and renunciation—"But he was sad at this word, and went away sorrowful, for he had great possessions" (Mark 10:22).

When he "heard that saying" (Matt. 19:22). When we hear a thing is not necessarily when it is spoken, but when we are in a state to listen to it and to understand. Our Lord's statements seem to be so simple and gentle, and they slip unobserved into the subconscious mind. Then something happens in our circumstances, and up comes one of these words into our consciousness and we hear it for the first time, and it makes us reel with amazement. This man, when he heard what Jesus said, understood what He meant. He did not dispute it, he did not argue; he heard it, and he went away expressionless with sorrow. There was no doubt as to what Jesus said, no debate as to what He meant, and it produced in him a sorrow that had no words. He found he had too big an interest in the other scale, and he drooped away from Jesus in sadness, not in rebellion.

The revelation and the riches—"And you will have treasure in heaven."

It is the trial of our faith that makes us wealthy in heaven. We want the treasure on earth all the time. We interpret answers to prayer on the material plane only, and if God does not answer there, we say He does not answer at all. Treasure in heaven is faith that has been tried, otherwise it is only possible gold. "Oh yes, I believe God can do everything." But have I proved that He can do one thing? If I have, the next time a trial of faith comes I can go through it smilingly because of the wealth in my heavenly banking account.

The regulation and the road—"And come . . . follow Me."

Come, follow Me, not find out the way, but, Come. You cannot come if there is any remnant of the wrong disposition in you because you are sure to want to direct God. "Come to Me" (Matt. 11:28), these words were spoken to those who had felt the appeal of the Highest, the aspiration, the longing, the master passion to be perfect. "Come to Me . . . and I will give you rest," stay you, poise you; "Take My yoke upon you and learn from Me . . . and you will find rest" (v. 29), all along the way. "If anyone desires to come after Me, let him deny himself, and take up his cross, and follow Me" (Matt. 16:24). The road is the way He went. "I will make the place of My feet glorious" (Isa. 60:13). Where is the place of His feet? Among the poor, the sick and sorrowful, among the bad and devil-possessed, among the hypocrites. And He says, "Follow Me"—there.

The Go of Sacramental Service

Matthew 5:41

Lord, I have fallen again—a human lump of earth!
Selfish I was, and heedless to offend;
Stood on my rights. Thy own child would not send
Away his shreds of nothing for the whole God!
Wretched, to thee who savest, low I bend:
Give me the power to let my rag-rights go
In the great wind that from thy gulf doth blow.

Keep me from wrath, let it seem ever so right:
My wrath will never work thy righteousness.
Up, up the hill, to the whiter than snow-shine,
Help me to climb, and dwell in pardon's light.
I must be pure as thou, or ever less
Than thy design of me—therefore incline
My heart to take men's wrongs as thou tak'st mine.

To go the second mile means always do your duty, and a great deal more than your duty, in a spirit of loving devotion that does not even know you have done it. If you are a saint the Lord will tax your walking capacity to the limit. The supreme difficulty is to go the second mile with God, because no one understands why you are being such a fool.

The summing up of our Lord's teaching is that it is impossible to carry out unless He has done a supernatural work in us. The Sermon on the Mount is not an ideal, because an ideal must have as its working power the possibility of its realization in the disposition obsessed by it. "Love your enemies" (Matt. 5:44); "Give to him who asks you" (Matt. 5:42); these things have no place in a person's natural disposition. Jesus Christ is the only One who can fulfill the Sermon on the Mount. We have to face ourselves with the teaching of Jesus and see that we do not wilt it away. The demands our Lord makes on His disciples are to be measured by His own character. The Sermon on the Mount is the statement of the working out in actuality of the disposition of Jesus Christ in the life of anyone.

Have we really come to the conclusion that if we are ever to be disciples it must be by being made disciples supernaturally? As long as we have the endeavor and the strain and the dead-set purpose of being disciples, it is almost certain we are not. Our Lord's making of a disciple is supernatural; He does not build on any natural capacity. "You did not choose Me, but I chose you" (John 15:16). That is always the way the grace of God begins to work, it is a constraint we cannot get away from. We can disobey it, but we cannot generate it. The drawing power is the supernatural grace of God and we can never trace where that work begins. We have to choose to obey, and He does all the rest. To face ourselves with the standards of Jesus produces not delight, but despair to begin with. But when we get to despair we are immediately willing to come to Jesus as paupers and to receive from Him. Despair is the initial gateway to delight in faith.

The Dangers of Intensity on Alien Ground

In our Lord's day the class known as Zealots hated the Roman dominance with an intensity of detestation; they would bow their heads and have their necks severed by the Roman sword rather than obey the tyrant. Just as the early disciples of Jesus were on alien ground politically, so as disciples of the Lord we are on alien ground in this world. The intensity of early devotion to Jesus must make for fanaticism to begin with. An intense person sees nothing, feels nothing, and does nothing unless it be violently.

There was a difference between the disciples of John the Baptist and the disciples of Jesus. John taught his disciples asceticism, there was no sociability about him. When Jesus came He was not marked by intense religious zeal in the way everyone else was. External intensities marked the religious age in which Jesus lived, but they did not mark Him. Our Lord did not identify Himself with the cause of the Zealots; He laid down His life as the Servant of Jehovah. We bring an alien atmosphere to the New Testament. Today many would sum up Jesus as an idle man.

The Direction by Impulse—In the training of the early disciples our Lord persistently checked impulse, and Peter, the most impulsive of them all, got rebuke after rebuke for obeying impulse. Watch how the Spirit of God checks whenever we obey impulse. His checks always bring a rush of self-conscious foolishness, and instantly we want to vindicate ourselves. Impulse must be disciplined into intuition. There was nothing of the nature of impulse about our Lord, nor of cold-bloodedness, but a calm strength that was never disturbed by panic. Most of us develop our Christianity along the line of our temperament, not along the line of God. To try and develop Christianity along the line of impulse is an impertinence when viewed alongside the strong Son of God. Some of us are like grasshoppers spiritually. Impulse is a natural trait in natural life, but in spiritual things our Lord absolutely checks it because it always hinders. Discipleship is built not on natural affinities but entirely on the supernatural grace of God. The one characteristic of discipleship is likeness to Jesus Christ.

The Dissipation of Impressions—All human beings have some kind of affinity for everything God has made. Our Lord deliberately reduces the impressions arising from these natural affinities until He gets the heart established in grace. In Luke 14:26, our Lord mentioned the closest affinities, all of which have been created by God, and yet He said there are times when you must hate them. Notice how your nature reacts when you listen to some of the stern teaching of the Bible. There is a feeling of outrage, and yet at the same time the certainty that it is right. God's original order was that there should be no sin, therefore every natural affinity could be indulged in; but sin entered in, and consequently when we become disciples the first thing we have to do is to cut off many affinities and live maimed lives.

In the Sermon on the Mount our Lord distinctly teaches the necessity of being maimed (See Matt. 5:29–30). If you are going to be spiritual, says Jesus, you must barter the natural—sacrifice it. If you say, "I do not want to sacrifice the natural for the spiritual," then, says Jesus, you must barter the spiritual. It is not a punishment, but an eternal principle. Be prepared to be maimed, to be a one-eyed faddist, until your heart gets established. It is this dissipation of impressions that makes many a would-be disciple a deserter. Our Lord's statements embrace the whole of the spiritual life from beginning to end, and in v. 48 of Matthew 5, He completes the picture He began to give in vv. 29–30: "Therefore you shall be perfect, just as your Father in heaven is perfect."

The Disposition of Interests—The interests of the Son of God and of the disciple are to be identical. How long it takes to manifest that identity depends on the private history of the disciple and his Lord.

Our Lord warns His disciples not to cast their pearls before swine. He is inculcating the need to examine carefully what we present of God's truth to others. If our Lord reduces our affinities and makes us live a maimed life in the meantime, it is at the peril of our spiritual lives if we try to explain it to others. Other people, seeing the limitations of the life, say what can there be wrong in this and in that? There is nothing wrong in them, but we know that it is at the peril of our lives with God that we touch them. The maimed life and the misunderstood life must go on.

Be prepared to be a limited fool in the sight of others, says Jesus, in order to further your spiritual character. We value the understanding of those we love most so much that Jesus has to take the last place. A disciple in the making may often tell Jesus that father or mother or friend or other interests must be heeded first, and the Lord administers no rebuke. The inevitable lesson is learned presently in a way in which it ought never to have had to be learned.

The Delays in Identification

Passionate, genuine affection for Jesus will lead to all sorts of vows and promises which it is impossible to fulfill. It is an attitude of mind and heart that sees only the heroic. We are called to be unobtrusive disciples, not heroes. When we are right with God the tiniest thing done out of love to Him is more precious to Him than any eloquent preaching of a sermon. We have introduced into our conception of Christianity heroic notions that come from paganism and not from the teaching of our Lord.

Jesus warned His disciples that they would be treated as nobodies; He never said they would be brilliant or marvelous. We all have a lurking desire to be exhibitions for God, to be put, as it were, in His show room. Jesus does not want us to be specimens, He wants us to be so taken up with Him that we never think about ourselves, and the only impression left on others by our lives is that Jesus Christ is having His unhindered way.

Peter . . . walked on the water to go to Jesus—Matt. 14:29

Walking on water is easy to impulsive pluck, but walking on dry land as a disciple of Jesus Christ is different. Peter walked on the water to go to Jesus, but he followed Him afar off on the land. We do not need the grace of God to stand crises; human nature and our pride will do it. We can buck up and face the music of a crisis magnificently, but it does require the supernatural grace of God to live twenty-four hours of the day as a saint, to go through drudgery as a saint, to go through poverty as a saint, to go through an ordinary, unobtrusive, ignored existence as a saint, unnoticed and unnoticeable. The "show business" which is so incorporated into our view of Christian work today has caused us to drift far from our Lord's conception of discipleship. It is instilled in us to think that we have to do exceptional things for God; we do not. We have to be exceptional in ordinary things, to be holy in mean streets, among mean people, surrounded by sordid sinners. That is not learned in five minutes.

Jesus took the early disciples in hand to train them, and at the end of three years of intimate companionship with Him, they all forsook Him and fled. Then they came to the end of themselves and all their self-sufficiency, and realized that if ever they were going to be different it must be by receiving a new Spirit. After the Resurrection Jesus "breathed on them, and said to them, 'Receive the Holy Spirit' " (John 20:22).

Do we really believe we need another Spirit? Are we basing our religious lives on our impulses, on our natural affections, on what other people take us for? Or are we based on what Jesus wants us to be? Jesus guides us by making us His friends.

Why can I not follow You now?—John 13:37

Determination and devotion, protestations and vows are all born of self-consciousness, and must die out of a disciple. A child never makes vows. We have to be so taken up with Jesus that we are never impudent enough to vow anything. All our vows and resolutions end in denial because we have no power to carry them out. Natural devotion will always deny Jesus Christ somewhere or other. Whenever the grace of God takes hold of us, we never think of vowing anything, we are lost in an amazing devotion which is not conscious.

The domination of self-consciousness has to be put to death—"I have vowed, I have promised, and I have consecrated." It all has to go until there is only one I, the Lord Jesus Christ.

What is that to you?—John 21:22

A disciple is one who minds neither his own business nor any one else's business, but looks steadfastly to Jesus and goes on following Him. We read books about the consecration of others, but it is as so much scaffolding. It all has to go and the time comes when there is only one thing left—following Jesus.

One of the severest lessons we get comes from our stubborn refusal to see that we must not interfere in other people's lives. It takes a long time to realize the danger of being an amateur Providence, interfering with God's order for others. We see a certain person suffering and we say, "He shall not suffer; I will see that he does not," and we put a hand straight in front of God's permissive will to prevent it, and He has to say, "What is that to you?"

All these things are elements in our identification with Jesus. How long it takes Him to get us identified with Him depends upon us. We cause delays to God by persistently doing things in our own way. He never gets impatient, He waits until everything has fallen away and there is nothing left but our identification with Him. To be absolutely centered in Jesus means that all things and all people are welcome alike to me, because they are all arranged for in their times and seasons by my heavenly Father.

The Discipline by Instruction in Apprehending Growth

Beware of continually wanting to be thrilled. In the natural world the one who is always wanting experiences of ecstasy and excitement is disappointingly unreliable, and the same is true in the spiritual world. There are unemployables in the spiritual domain, spiritually decrepit people who refuse to do anything unless they are supernaturally inspired.

His Cross—"Him they compelled to bear His cross" (Matt. 27:32).

Simon the Cyrenian, in unwillingly fulfilling the instruction given in the Sermon on the Mount, unconsciously points out the lesson to us that we must be identified with the Cross of Christ before ever we can carry our own crosses.

His cup—"You will indeed drink My cup" (Matt. 20:23).

This is not the cup of martyrdom, for our Lord was not a martyr. We must be identified with the atoning death of our Lord before we can be disciples. Many of us want to be disciples but we do not want to come by way of His atoning death; we do not want to be compelled to be orthodox to the Cross of Christ, to drink the cup that He drank. But there is no other way. We must be regenerated, supernaturally made all over again, before we can be His disciples.

His confession—"Behold, we are going up to Jerusalem" (Luke 18:31).

This is the mightiest word on discipleship that our Lord ever spoke, for Jerusalem was the place where He reached the climax of His Father's will for Him, and He identifies us with Himself in our going up to our Jerusalem.

We have become so taken up with the idea of being prepared for something in the future that is the conception we have of discipleship. It is true, but it is also untrue. The attitude of the Christian life is that we must be prepared now, this second; this is the time. What we are in relation to Jesus, not what we do or say for Him, gives His heart satisfaction and furthers His kingdom. "Therefore whoever confesses Me before men" (Matt. 10:32), said Jesus. The word confess means that every particle of our nature says the same thing, not our mouths only, but the very makeup of our flesh and blood, confesses that Jesus Christ has come in the flesh (see 1 John 4:2).

It is easy to talk, easy to have fine thoughts; but none of that means being a disciple. Being a disciple is to be something that is an infinite satisfaction to Jesus every minute, whether in secret or in public.

What Is a Missionary?

Yet it was well, and Thou hast said in season
    As is the Master shall the servant be:
Let me not subtly slide into treason,
    Seeking an honour which they gave not Thee:

Never at even, pillowed on a pleasure,
    Sleep with the wings of aspiration furled,
Hide the last mite of the forbidden treasure,
    Keep for my joys a world within the world.

He as He wills shall solder and shall sunder,
    Slay in a day and quicken in an hour,
Tune Him a chorus from the Sons of Thunder,
    Forge and transform my passion into power.

Ay, for this Paul, a scorn and a reviling,
    Weak as you know him and the wretch you see,
Even in these eyes shall ye behold His smiling,
    Strength in infirmities and Christ in me.

The Sure Characteristics
John 17:18, 20:21–23

The great danger in missionary enterprise is that God's call may be effaced by the needs of the people until human sympathy overwhelms altogether the significance of Jesus Christ's sending. "As the Father has sent Me, I also send you" (John 20:21). A missionary is a saved and sanctified soul detached to Jesus. The one thing that must not be overlooked is the personal relationship to Jesus Christ and to His point of view; if that is overlooked, the needs are so great, the conditions so perplexing, that every power of mind and heart will fail and falter. We are apt to forget that the great reason for missionary enterprise is not first the elevation of the people, nor first the education of the people, nor even first the salvation of the people, but first and foremost the command of Jesus Christ, "Go therefore and make disciples of all the nations" (Matt. 28:19).

If we are going to remain true to the Bible's conception of a missionary, we must go back to the source. A missionary is one sent by Jesus Christ as He was sent by the Father. The great, dominating note is not first the needs of humanity, but the command of Jesus Christ. Consequently the real source of inspiration is always behind, never in front. Today the tendency is to put the inspiration in front of us and bring it all out in accordance with our conception of success. In the New Testament the inspiration is behind, that is, the Lord Jesus Christ Himself. We are called to be true to Him, to be faithful to Him, to carry out His enterprises.

In reviewing the lives of men and women of God and the history of the Church of God there is a tendency to say, "How wonderfully astute those people were! How perfectly they understood what God wanted of them." The truth is that the astute mind behind these men and women was not a human mind at all, but the mind of God. We give credit to human wisdom when we should give credit to the divine guidance of God through child-like people. They were foolish enough in the eyes of the world to trust God's wisdom and supernatural equipping, while watching carefully their own steadfast relationship to Him.

The New Testament lays down clearly what the work of the missionary is: it is to disciple all nations according to the command of the risen Lord. The method of missions is clearly stated in each of the four Gospels. Matthew records the farewell command which Jesus gave to His disciples, and that command is to teach, to disciple all the nations, not to make converts to our ways of thinking but to make disciples of Jesus. In Mark's gospel the method is defined as preaching the gospel to every creature, accompanied by the power to cast out devils and to speak with new tongues. In Luke's gospel the method is described as preaching repentance and remission of sins to all the nations. In John's gospel the method is described by our Lord as feeding His sheep and tending His lambs. The methods through which the life-giving truth is to be presented are as varied as the needs and conditions of the nations among whom the missionaries are placed.

Jesus Christ did not say go and save souls; the salvation of souls is God's work. Jesus told the disciples to go and teach—disciple—all nations. The salvation of souls comes about through the ministry of God's Word and the proclaiming of redemption by God's servants; but the command to the missionary is to disciple those who are saved. Every now and again the church becomes content with seeing people saved. When people get saved the disciple's work begins, and the great point about discipling is that you can never make a disciple unless you are one yourself. When the disciples came back from their first mission they were filled with joy and said, "Lord, even the demons are subject to us in Your name" (Luke 10:17). And Jesus said in effect, "Don't rejoice in successful service, but rejoice that you are rightly related to God through Me." Those who remain true to the call of God are those whose lives are stamped and sealed by God; they have one great purpose underneath, and that is to disciple men and women to Jesus.

The Subject Matter
Luke 24:45–48

The subject matter of missions is the life and death and resurrection of Jesus Christ for one purpose, "that repentance and remission of sins should be preached in His name to all nations" (Luke 24:47). The subject matter of missions remains an unchangeable truth, an historic fact, "the Lamb slain from the foundation of the world" (Rev. 13:8).

The Cross as it is manifested in the life of our Lord is not the cross of a martyr. He came on purpose to die. When we get away from the teaching of the New Testament, the first thing that happens is that sin is minimized and the meaning of the Cross of Christ departed from. The Cross of Jesus Christ is the historic manifestation of the inherent nature of the Trinity. Through all the ages the perplexity in the minds of those without the Spirit of God arises because the Bible presents something utterly unlike what the natural heart thinks it wants. The natural mind thinks of God in a circle—everything is going to evolve and develop in a plain, simple way. According to the Bible things do not go as we expect them to, either in individual life or in history, but always at cross purposes. The symbol of the nature of God is not a circle, complete and self-centered; the symbol of God's nature is the Cross. The end God has in view is entirely different from that arrived at by people's unaided thinking.

For instance, the conception that is working like leaven today all though missionary enterprise is that we are going to evolve into a circle of brilliant success. The great conflict that awaits the missionary today is the conflict against the evolutionary idea that everything is growing better. The Bible does not look forward to an evolution of humanity; the Bible talks of a revolution: "Do not marvel that I said to you, 'You must be born again' " (John 3:7). We have to get back to the preaching of the Cross and the remission of sins through the death of our Lord.

The Scriptural Method
John 21:15–17

The method here is described by our Lord as feeding His lambs and tending His sheep. Continually we get to the place where we see no one as sinful because we do not want to become shepherds. The great challenge is made to the missionary, not that people are difficult to reclaim, not that there is callous indifference on the part of people to the message; the challenge is to my faith in my Lord—do I believe He is able? Our Lord seems to come steadily to us in every individual case we meet and ask, "Do you believe that I am able to do this?" (Matt. 9:28).

Whether it be a case of demon possession, bodily upset, mental twist, backsliding, indifference, difference of nationality and thought, the challenge is to me. Do I know my risen Lord? Do I know the power of His indwelling Spirit? Am I wise enough in God's sight, and foolish enough according to the wisdom of the world to bank on what Jesus has told me? Or am I abandoning the supernatural position, which is the only one for a missionary, of boundless confidence in Jesus? If we take up any other method we depart altogether from the scriptural method laid down by our Lord, "All authority has been given to Me. . . . Go therefore."

Every time God presents us with a problem in Christian work He gives us something to match it in our own hearts, and if we will let His power work there we shall go forth with unshakable confidence in what He can do for anyone. If we know in our own lives that God can do what Jesus Christ said He could, we can never be put in the place where we will be discouraged. We may be put in the heart of the vilest and most terrible phases of degeneracy but we can never be discouraged, nor can we be defiled, because we have the very nature of God in us and we are kept like the light, unsullied.

The Special Persons
Matt. 16:18

This is our Lord's statement as to what constitutes membership in His church—a revelation of who He is and the public confession of it. No one knows who Jesus Christ is but by the Spirit of God, and the fact that one knows who Jesus is and makes confession of it is the bedrock on which Christ builds His church, according to His own Word. The special person called to do missionary work is every person who is a member of the church of Christ. The call does not come to a chosen few, it is to every one of us. The special call is to stay at home. The big call remains Go, and if I am staying I have to give God the reason.

According to our Lord there is not a home church and a foreign church, it is all one great work beginning at home and then going elsewhere, "beginning at Jerusalem" (Luke 24:47). Jerusalem was not the home of the disciples; Jerusalem was the place where our Lord was rejected. "Begin there," said Jesus. In His first sermon at Nazareth our Lord said that it was God's way to send His message by strangers before it was accepted, and the history of the Church has proved that it is out of the mouth of strangers that the great awakenings have always come. Take any country that has had the life of God introduced into it, it has never been introduced by those belonging to the country, but always from the outside.

In our Lord's conception all the world is the same to God, and the command to go embraces us all. Missionaries are ordained to preach, trained to teach and to heal, skilled to win savage races for Christ. But every method is to be subordinated to the one great message of the remission of sins through faith in His blood (Romans 3:25–26).

Whatever line the missionary takes, whether it be medical or educational, there is only one purpose; one great truth grips and sends forth and holds so that there is nothing else on earth to live for but to proclaim the death of Christ for the remission of sins. The note of false missionary enterprise leaves out the fundamental purpose of evangelization and says that civilization must come first. Robert Moffatt uttered solemn words when he said he little thought he would live to see the day when earnest missionaries would reverse the order of God, when the watchword would not be to evangelize first, but to civilize. Our Lord illustrated this in His parable (see Matt. 13:32). The birds of civilization come and lodge in the branches of the spiritual tree and people say, "Now this is what is to be!" and they have not seen God's purpose at all. If we do not see God's purpose we shall continually be misled by externals.

The thing to watch in all our enterprise for God is lest we should get swamped out of personal relationship to Jesus Christ, the One who gives us the command Go. "I have become all things to all men," said Paul, "that I might by all means save some" (1 Cor. 9:22).

The one dominating purpose and passion at the heart of the missionary is his or her own personal relationship to Jesus Christ. A missionary is a construction made through the Atonement by the God who made the universe. It is not a sentiment, it is true that God spoils a man or woman for any other use in the world except for one thing only, to win souls to Jesus and to disciple them in His name. The saddest thing is to see a person who gave great promise of being a power for God in the world fizzle out like an extinct volcano. The reason for it is that a rational, common sense explanation of holy things has ruthlessly torn down the great scriptural idea at the heart of the life. Consequently the life has withered and become a negligible quantity from God's standpoint.

Thank God for the words of our Lord, "He who believes in Me . . . out of his heart will flow rivers of living water" (John 7:38). Always remain true to the Fountainhead.

Missionary Munitions

During World War I the Minister of Munitions said that everything depended on the workshops of Britain. What was true in the enormous world crisis of war is symbolically true in work for God. But what are the workshops that supply the munitions for God's enterprises? The workshop of missionary munitions is the hidden, personal, worshiping life of the saint.

Worshiping as Occasion Serves
John 1:48

The constant, private habit of the life of the missionary ought to be worshiping as occasion serves, that is the first great essential for fitness. The time will come when no more "fig tree" life is possible; when we are right out in the open and glare of the work, and we shall find ourselves without any value if we have not been worshiping God as occasion serves. We imagine we would be all right if a big crisis arose; but the crisis only reveals the stuff we are made of; it does not put anything into us.

"If God gives the call of course I shall rise to the occasion." You will not unless you have risen to the occasion in the workshop. If you are not the real article before God there, doing the duty that lies nearest, instead of being revealed as fit for God when the crisis comes, you will be revealed as unfit. Crises always reveal character until it is revealed to us.

If you do not worship as occasion serves at home you will be of no use in the foreign field; but if you put the worship of God first, and get the revelation of who God is, then when the call comes you will be ready for it. In the unseen life under the fig tree, the life which no one saw but God, you have been learning and preparing, and now when the strain comes you are perfectly fit to be relied on by God. Worshiping is greater than work in that it absorbs work.

"And He said to him, 'Most assuredly, I say to you, hereafter you shall see heaven open, and the angels of God ascending and descending upon the Son of Man' " (John 1:51). Our Lord is the One in whom God and the individual can meet as one. If that has never been learned in our private worshiping life it will never be realized in active public work. "There is no need for this private worship of God. I cannot be expected to live the sanctified life in the circumstances I am in. There is no time for praying just now, no time for Bible reading. When I get out into the work and opportunity comes for all that, of course I shall be all right." If you have not been worshiping as occasion serves you will not only be useless when you get out into service but a tremendous hindrance to those who are associated with you. Imagine a general having ammunition made in a workshop at the back of the trenches. His soldiers would be blown up while attempting it. Yet that is what we seem to expect to do in work for God.

Ministering as Opportunity Surrounds
John 13:14–15

Ministering as opportunity surrounds does not mean selecting our surroundings, but being very selectly God's in any haphazard surroundings He may engineer for us. The characteristics we exhibit in our immediate surroundings are an indication of what we shall be like in other circumstances by and by.

"Jesus, knowing that the Father had given all things into His hands, and that He had come from God and was going to God" (John

13:3). We might have expected the record to go on, He was transfigured before them, but the next thing we read that our Lord did was of the most menial, commonplace order. He "took a towel and girded Himself . . . and began to wash the disciples' feet" (vv. 4–5).

Can we use a towel as our Lord did? Towels and basins and feet and sandals, all the ordinary, sordid things of our lives, reveal more quickly than anything what we are made of. It is not the big occasions that reveal us, but the little occasions. It takes God Incarnate to do the most menial commonplace things properly.

"If I then, your Lord and Teacher, have washed your feet, you also ought to wash one another's feet" (v. 14). Our Lord did not say, "I have the means of the salvation of thousands, I have been the most successful in My service, now you go and do the same thing." He said: "I have washed your feet; you go and wash one another's feet." We try to get out of it by washing the feet of those who do not belong to our own set—we will wash the unbeliever's feet, or feet in the slums, but fancy washing my brother's feet, my wife's, my husband's, the feet of the minister of my church! Our Lord said—one another's feet.

Watch the humor of our heavenly Father. It is seen in the way He brings across our paths the type of person who exhibits to us what we have been like to Him. "Now," He says, "show that one the same love that I have shown you." If Jesus Christ has lifted us in love and grace, we must show that love to someone else. It is of no use to say, "Oh, I will do all that when I get out to the field." The only way to produce the munitions for God's enterprises is to minister as opportunity surrounds us now, and God will surround us with ample opportunity of doing to others as He has done to us.

The workshop for missionary munitions on which God draws for His work is the private lives of those who are not only saved and sanctified by Him, but who immediately begin to minister where they are. We read of Peter's wife's mother that when Jesus touched her, "immediately she arose and served them"; a perfect and complete deliverance, and immediate service. There was no interesting convalescent stage. Some people do not like to get saved all of a sudden, they do not like to have their problems solved in a lightning flash; they prefer to be spiritual sponges and mop up all the sympathy they can. Peter's wife's mother is the type of the life in which God has done His work. In the full and amazing strength of God, she arose and did what lay nearest, and went on as if she had never been ill.

Graduating as Obligations Separate
Matt. 11:28–29

In Matt 11:29, Jesus said, "Take My yoke upon you and learn from Me," the graduating course in the training school of our Lord. Many of us get as far as verse 28, "Come to Me," then come the obligations which separate us from all else, and we have to enter into the discipline of fellowship. We have to take upon us His yoke, and see that we bow our necks to no other yoke; then when the strain comes, we can go through anything.

"Learn from Me, for I am gentle and lowly in heart." We say readily, "Of course Jesus was meek and lowly," but was He? Read the account of the cleansing of the temple; where is the meek and mild and gentle Jesus there? He "made Himself of no reputation" (Phil. 2:7), but when His Father's honor was touched, all was different. The meekness and lowliness of our Lord is seen in His relationship to His Father; He never murmured at anything His Father brought, and never gave way to self-pity.

That is meekness and lowliness of heart we need to learn, and we shall never learn it unless redemption of our Lord has been at work in us, completely restoring and emancipating us, and getting us into yoke with Him. If we have taken His yoke upon us, we shall never say when things are difficult, "Why should this happen to me?" We shall be meek toward God's dispensations for us as Jesus was meek towards His Father.

"And you will find rest for your souls" (Matt. 11:29), you will make the continual discovery of the undisturbedness of heart which is the delight of those who "follow the Lamb wherever He goes" (Rev. 14:4).

The workshop of missionary munitions is the temple of the Holy Spirit, our actual bodily lives. "Do you not know that you are the temple of God?" (1 Cor. 3:16).

The Missionary's Master

To have a master and to be mastered are not the same thing, but diametrically opposed. If I have the idea that I am being mastered, it is a sure proof that I have no master. If I feel I am in subjection to someone, then I may be sure that someone is not the one I love. To have a master means to have one who is closer than a friend, one whom I know knows me better than I know myself, one who has fathomed the remotest abyss of my heart and satisfied it, one who brings me the secure sense that he has met and solved every perplexity of my mind—that, and nothing less, is to have a master.

Jesus Christ is the Master of the missionary. The conception of mastership that we get from human life is totally different from the mastership of Jesus. If I have the idea that I am being mastered by Jesus, then I am far from being in the relationship to Himself He wants me to be in, a relationship where He is easily Master without my conscious knowledge of it. All I am aware of is that I am His to obey.

Our Lord never takes measures to make us obey Him. Our obedience is the outcome of a oneness of spirit with Him through His redemption. That is why, whenever our Lord talked about discipleship, He prefaced it with an if. "You do not need to unless you like," but "If anyone desires to come after Me, let him deny himself" (Matt. 16:24), deny his independence, give up his right to himself, to Me. Our Lord is not talking about one's position hereafter, but about being of value to Him in this order of things.

Human authority always insists on obedience; our Lord never does. He makes His standard very clear, and if the relation of the spirit within me is that of love to Him, then I do all He says without any hesitation. If I begin to hesitate and to debate, it is because I love someone else in competition with Him—myself. The only word by which to describe mastership in experience is love: "If you love Me, keep My commandments" (John 14:15).

Obedience to Jesus Christ is essential, but not compulsory. He never insists on being Master. We feel that if only He would insist, we would obey Him. But our Lord never enforces His thou shalts and thou shalt nots. He never takes means to force us to do what He says; He never coerces. In certain moods we wish He would make us do the thing, but He will not; and in other moods we wish He would leave us alone altogether, but He will not. If we do not keep His commandments He does not come and tell us we are wrong; we know it, we cannot get away from it. There is no ambiguity in our minds as to whether what He says is right. Our Lord never says you must, but if we are to be His disciples we know we must.

Christianity is not a "sanctified" anything; it is the life of Jesus manifested in our mortal flesh by the miracle of His redemption, and that will mean that whenever a crisis comes Jesus is instantly seen to be a Master without a moment's hesitation; there is no debate.

"You call Me Teacher and Lord, and you say well, for so I am" (John 13:13)—but is He? The great consciousness in the mind of our Lord is that He is our Master, and we, too, have to come into this consciousness. Master and Lord have very little place in our spiritual vocabulary; we prefer the words Savior and Sanctifier and Healer. In other words, we know very little about love as Jesus revealed it. It is seen in the way we use the word *obey*. Our use of the word implies the submission of an inferior to a superior; obedience in our Lord's use of the word is the relationship of equals, a child and its father; "Though He was a Son, yet He learned obedience by the things which He suffered"

(Heb. 5:8). Our Lord was not a servant of God, He was His Son. The Son's obedience as Redeemer was because He is Son, not in order to be Son.

The Master Physician

"So He touched her hand, and the fever left her. And she arose and served them" (Matt. 8:15).

These words crystallize for us the revelation of our Lord as the Master Physician. When He touches there is no convalescence. Unless the missionary is one who has been touched by the Master Physician, his or her touch may be one of skill but not of supreme healing. When our Lord is the Master of His disciples He conveys His effectual touch through them to others.

Touch has more power than even speech to convey the personality. If some people touch us, we feel the worse for it for days. If others touch us, we live transfigured lives for days. That is an experience recognizable by us all, but we may not have realized that it is because the touch conveys the dominating personality behind. A caress from a bad personality is incarnated hypocrisy. It is at grave peril to our own souls that we ignore these subtle indications of warning. When the barriers that God creates around His children are broken down and His warnings ignored, we shall find that the Enemy will break through at the places we have broken down. If we keep in touch with the Master He will keep us out of touch with badness.

The Master touch of our Lord breaks the fever of self, and life is profoundly altered. When our Lord is the Master, no matter where the disciple goes, His touch comes through that person all the time. "A woman . . . touched the hem of His garment" (Matt. 9:20). The missionary is, as it were, the hem of

His garment and virtue goes out through the garment's hem to the needy one who touched.

The Master Artist

"Then He touched their eyes, saying, 'According to your faith let it be to you' " (Matt. 9:29).

The Master Touch produces sight.

In human sight the thing we soon lose is what Ruskin called "the innocence of the eye." An artist records exactly from this innocence of sight, he does not bring in his logical faculties and interfere with what he sees by telling himself what he ought to see. Most of us know what we are looking at and instead of trusting the innocence of sight, we confuse it by trying to tell ourselves what we see. If ever you have been taught by anyone to see, you will know what this means. Drummond says that Ruskin taught him to see. An artist does not tell us what he sees, he enables us to see; he communicates the unutterable identity of what he sees. It is a great thing to see with anyone. Jesus never tells us what to see, but when His touch is upon our eyes we know that we see what He is seeing, He restores this pristine innocence of sight. "Unless one is born again, he cannot see the kingdom of God" (John 3:3).

An artist conveys personality by means of the medium and creates wonderful things, and if the Master touch has given the missionary sight God can do wonderful things through him or her. Paul was sent by God to "open their eyes, in order to turn them from darkness to light" (Acts 26:18).

A skilled artist does not need to use more than two or three colors; an amateur requires all the tubes in the box squirted out like a condensed rainbow. The Master Artist used strange things to open blind eyes—spittle, clay, and water from a pool, but remember He used them, and He produced the miracle of sight.

The missionary may easily be looked on as one of the despised things, but if used by Jesus, he or she will produce sight in others.

The Master Musician

"And He touched his ear, and healed him" (Luke 22:51).

When the Master touch comes on the sick or the sightless or the deaf, the miracle of the personality is conveyed at once. Touch conveys the personality to the flesh and to the sight, and sound conveys the personality to the hearing. It is personality that gives to sound, which is amoral, its moral or immoral character. There is some music, for instance, that we listen to at the peril of our souls because of the personality behind it. Those who are healed by the Master Musician have the personality of God conveyed to them. When we have been ravished with the wonder of the Master Musician's music, He gives us a badly tuned instrument to put into repair for Him.

The Master Speaker

"And He took him aside from the multitude . . . and touched his tongue" (Mark 7:33–35).

This incident is one of many that reveal the unique use of speech by our Lord. "Then, looking up to heaven, He sighed, and said to him, Ephphatha, that is, 'Be opened' " (v. 34). The tongue was in its right place in our Lord; He only used it to speak the words of God, He never spoke from His right to Himself. "The words that I speak to you I do not speak on My own authority; but the Father who dwells in Me, does the works" (John 14:10). The words Jesus spoke were the exact expression of the thought of God. "And the Word was God" (John 1:1).

The Master Speaker, after conveying His life to us by means of His words, turns us loose into a tower of Babel and tells us to speak His messages there. Missionaries are those whom Jesus Christ has taken aside from the multitude, and, having put His fingers into their ears and touched their tongues, has sent them straight forth from hearing their Master, with their own tongues loosened and their speech plain, to speak "all the words of this life" (Acts 5:20).

The Missionary's Way

"I am the way, the truth, and the life" (John 14:6).

However far we may drift we must always come back to these words of our Lord: "I am the way," not a road that we leave behind us, but the way itself. Jesus Christ is the way of God, not a way that leads to God; that is why He says, "Come to Me" (Matt. 11:28), "Abide in Me" (John 15:4).

"I am the truth," not the truth about God, not a set of principles, but the truth itself. Jesus Christ is the Truth of God. "No one comes to the Father except through Me" (John 14:6). We can get to God as Creator in other ways, but no one can come to God as Father in any other way than by Jesus Christ (See Matt. 11:27).

"I am the life." Jesus Christ is the Life of God as He is the Way and the Truth of God. Eternal life is not a gift from God, it is the gift of God Himself. The life imparted to me by Jesus is the life of God. "He who has the Son has life" (1 John 5:12); "I have come that they may have life" (John 10:10); "And this is eternal life, that they may know You, the only true God" (John 17:3). We have to abide in the way; to be incorporated into the truth; to be infused by the life.

The Conditions of the Way

"Let this mind be in you which was also in Christ Jesus" (Phil 2:5).

Paul goes on to state the characteristics of the mind which we are to form, that is, the mind which was in Christ Jesus when

84

He was on this earth, utterly self-effaced and self-emptied—not the mind of Christ when He was in glory. We receive the mind of Christ when He was in glory. We receive the Spirit of Christ as a gift but we do not receive His mind; we have to construct that and this is done in the same way that we construct the natural mind—by the way our disposition reacts when we come in contact with external things. Mind, or soul, is the way the personal spirit expresses itself in the body. We have to lose our own way of thinking and form Jesus Christ's way. "By your patience possess your souls" (Luke 21:19). It takes time and discipline. When we are regenerated and have the life of the Son of God in us God engineers our circumstances in order that we may form the mind of Christ.

Of exaltation—"Who, being in the form of God, did not consider it robbery to be equal with God" (Phil. 2:7).

Our Lord's exaltation was His equality with the Father. In the Christian life there are stages of experience that are exalted, times when we know what it is to live in the heavenly places in Christ Jesus, when we seem to be more on the mount than anywhere else. But we are not made for the mountain, we are made for the valley. We are made for the actual world not for the ideal world, but to be so in communion with the ideal that we can work it out in the actual and make it real. There is no life like the life of a missionary for bringing the ideal and the actual together. "Come to Me . . . and I will give you rest" (Matt. 11:28), said Jesus; "I will bring the ideal and the actual into one."

Of subordination—"But emptied Himself" (Phil. 2:7, RSV)

Our Lord annihilated Himself from His former exaltation and "taking the form of a bondservant, and coming in the likeness of men . . . He humbled Himself and became obedient to the point of death, even the death of the cross" (Phil. 2:7-8). Our Lord by

His own choice emptied Himself of all His former glory; and if we are to enter into fellowship with Him, we must deliberately go through the annihilation, not of glory, but of our right to ourselves in every shape and form. Our Lord's former condition was one of absolute equality with God. Our former condition is one of absolute independence of God.

"Let him deny himself" (Matt. 16:24), says Jesus. It is easy to do it in theory, easy to count all things but loss. Paul says he not only counted all things but loss, he "suffered the loss of all things" (Phil. 3:8), that He might win Christ. It is a sad thing to only come the length of counting the loss and say, "Oh yes, I see it will cost me my right to myself, it will cost me the world, it will cost me everything; but I do not intend to experience the loss. These things sound all right in the ideal, but they hit a bit too hard in the actual."

Of sanctification—"And for their sakes I sanctify Myself" (John 17:19).

The idea of sanctification as our Lord here uses it is the separation of holiness to God's use and for God's purpose. Our Lord separated His holy self to God. This idea of sanctification worked out in a missionary's life means more than the fact that one is personally identified with the Lord; it means that one deliberately sets apart one's sanctified self for God. The experience of sanctification is usually presented as a personal identification with Jesus Christ by which He "became for us . . . sanctification" (1 Cor. 1:30); the sanctification our Lord refers to is the sanctification of that sanctification. Beware of the idea of sanctification that makes a person say, "Now I am sanctified I can do what I like." To do so is immoral. "Even Christ did not please Himself" (Rom. 15:3). If our experience of sanctification ends in pious sentiment, the reason is that it has never dawned on us that we must deliberately set our sanctified selves apart for God's use as Jesus did.

The Commission of the Way

"As the Father has sent Me, I also send you" (John 20:21).

Our Lord's first obedience was not to the needs of people, not to the consideration of where He would be most useful, but to the will of His Father. "Behold, I have come . . . to do Your will, O God" (Heb. 10:7). And the first obedience of the missionary is to the will of our Lord. "You call me Teacher and Lord and you say well, for so I am" (John 13:13), but does it mean any more to us than the mere saying of it? "If I then, your Lord and Teacher, have washed your feet, you also ought to wash one another's feet" (v. 14), and we cannot do it by sentiment. It was in the hour when Jesus, "knowing that the Father had given all things into His hands, and that He had come from God, and was going to God" (John 13:3), began to wash the disciples' feet; and it is when we realize our union with Jesus Christ as our Lord and Master that we shall follow His example. It takes God Incarnate to do the meanest duty as it ought to be done. When Jesus touched things that were sordid and ordinary, He transfigured them.

The witness—John 8:18–19, 15:27.

Just as our Lord was a witness who satisfied His Father, so a Christian witness is one who satisfies his Master. "You shall be witnesses to Me" (Acts 1:8), not "witnesses to what I can do, but witnesses who satisfy Me in any circumstances I put you in. I reckon on you for extreme service, with no complaining on your part and no explanation on Mine." Being a martyr does not necessarily involve being a witness, but being a witness will involve martyrdom.

The Word—John 14:10, 17:8.

Our Lord said that His Word was not His own, but His Father's. Jesus never spoke from His right to Himself. "The

words that I speak to you I do not speak on my own authority"
(John 14:10). Jesus Christ is the Word of God in His own
person; He spoke the words of God with a human tongue, and
He has given to His disciples the words the Father gave to Him.
The disciple not only has to speak the words of God with his or
her tongue, but to bear the evidence of being a word of the Son,
as Jesus was the Word of God. To confess Christ means to say,
not only with the tongue, but with every bit of our lives, that
Jesus has come into our flesh. The Son was the exact expression
of the Father, and the saint must be an exact expression of the
Son.

The work—John 9:4, 14:12. "I must work the works of Him who
sent Me" (John 9:4).

According to our Lord the need is never the call. The need
is the opportunity; the call is the call of God. The call of God is
like the call of the sea, or of the mountains, or of the ice fields; no
one hears those calls who has not the nature of the sea or of the
mountains or of the ice fields within; and no one hears the call of
God who has not the nature of the Almighty within. If we have
received the nature of God, then we begin slowly to discern what
God wants us to do. Never have the idea that your discernment
of the need is the call. The need is the opportunity which will
prove whether you are worthy of the call. Because you realize a
need you have no right to say "I must go." If you are sanctified,
you cannot go unless you are sent.

The Conflict of the Way

"If the world hates you, you know that it hated Me
before it hated you" (John 15:18).

Our Lord told His disciples over and over again that they
must lay their account with the hatred of the world.

Of contrast—Matt. 10:16. In this verse our Lord gives the vivid contrast of sheep and wolves, of doves and serpents, and He uses the contrast in a particular connection—that of proclaiming His gospel.

Of contumely—Matt. 10:17–20. If these verses are unfamiliar to us today, it is because we are out of the center of identification with our Lord's purposes and are seeking to bring Him into our enterprises; but as surely as we are in fellowship with Him, we shall find the terrible and unpalatable truth expressed in these verses to be a very actual portion.

Of courage—Matt. 10:22–24. The courage our Lord alludes to here is that born in a heart in vivid relationship to Himself, compelling the body to perform the will of God even at the cost of death. Our Lord makes little of physical death but He makes much of moral and spiritual death.

The Consolations of the Way

"I will not leave you orphans; I will come to you" (John 14:18).

The consolations of the ways are not the sympathies of human sensibilities, but the great sustaining of the personal Holy Spirit.

Of love—John 17:26. The first mighty name for the consolations of the way is love, "That the love with which You loved Me may be in them." It is the Holy Spirit who brings this consolation. He sheds abroad the love of God in our hearts, the nature of God as exhibited in Jesus, with its impenetrable reserves. No human being can pump up what is not there. The consolation of love is not that of exquisite human understanding. It is the real nature of

God holding the individual life in effectual rectitude and effectual communion in the face of anything that may ever come.

Of joy—John 15:11. Joy is not happiness; joy is the result of the perfect fulfillment of the purpose of the life. We never want praise if we have done perfectly what we ought to do; we only want praise if we are not sure whether we have done well.

Jesus did not want praise; He did not need it, and He said "that My joy may remain in you" (John 15:11). The joy of Jesus Christ was in the absolute self-surrender and self-sacrifice of Himself to His Father, the joy of doing what the Father sent Him to do—"I delight to do Your will" (Ps. 40:8), and that is the joy He prays may be in His disciples. It is not a question of trying to work as Jesus did, but of having the personal presence of the Holy Spirit who works in us the nature of Jesus. One of the consolations of the way is the fathomless joy of the Holy Spirit manifesting itself in us as it did in the Son of God in the days of His flesh.

Of peace—John 14:27. The peace Jesus refers to here is not the peace of a conscience at rest, but the peace that characterized His own life. "My peace I give to you." His peace is a direct gift through the personal presence of the Holy Spirit.

The Consummation of the Way

"We will come to him, and make Our home with him" (John 14:23).

Jesus says that the relationship between the Father and the Son is to be the relationship between the Father and the Son and the sanctified soul.

Oneness—John 17:22. "That they may be one just as We are one."

Are we as close to Jesus Christ as that? God will not leave us alone until we are. There is one prayer that God must answer, and that is the prayer of Jesus.

Sovereignty—Matt. 19:28–29. Peter in his epistle says that we are to be "a royal priesthood" (1 Peter 2:9). The sovereignty alluded to by Peter, and by our Lord in these verses, is ultimately to be a literal sovereignty as well as a spiritual sovereignty.

Glory—John 17:22. "The glory which You gave Me I have given them."

What was the glory that Jesus had when He was Son of Man? It was not an external glory; Jesus effaced the Godhead in Himself so effectually that those without the Spirit of God despised Him. His glory was the glory of actual holiness and that is the glory He says He gives to the saint. The glory of the saint is the glory of actual holiness manifested in actual life here and now. There is a glory that the saint is only to behold, "that they may behold My glory which You have given me" (v. 24). What is that glory? "For You loved Me before the foundation of the world." That glory we are not to share but to behold. The word glory here must be understood in the same sense as the word form in Phil. 2:6. It refers to the absolute relation of deity that the Son of God had before He became incarnate.

The consummation of the missionary's way is centered in John 14:23: "We will come to him, and make Our home with him"—the triune God abiding with the saint.

Missionary Predestinations

Isaiah 49:1–2

This passage refers to the whole nation of Israel, to our Lord Jesus Christ, and to every individual saint.

The Election of Perfect Fitness for God

God created the people known as Israel for one purpose, to be the servants of Jehovah until through them every nation came to know who Jehovah was. The nation created for the service of Jehovah failed to fulfill God's predestination for it; then God called out a remnant, and the remnant failed; then out of the remnant came One who succeeded, the One whom we know as the Lord Jesus Christ. The Savior of the world came of this nation. He is called "the Servant of God" because He expresses exactly the creative purpose of God for the historic people of God. Through that one Man the purpose of God for the individual, for the chosen nation, and for the whole world is to be fulfilled. It is through Him that we are "a royal priesthood" (1 Pet. 2:9).

When this election to God in Christ Jesus is realized by us individually, God begins to destroy our prejudices and our parochial notions and to turn us into the servants of His own purpose. The experience of salvation in individual lives means the incoming of this realization of the election of God. When we are born from above we understand what is incomprehensible to human reason—that the predestination of God and our infinitesimal lives are made one and the same by Him. From the standpoint of rationalism that is nonsense; but it is revelation fact. The connection between the election of God and human free will is confusing to our Gentile type of mind, but the connection was an essential element underlying all Hebrew thought. The predestination of God cannot be experienced by individuals of their own free choice; but when we are born again the fact that we do choose what has been predestined of God comes to us as a revelation.

The rationalist says it is absurd to imagine that the purposes of Almighty God are furthered by an individual life, but it is true. God's predestinations are the voluntary choosing of the sanctified soul. One way in which the realization works out with us personally is when we say, "The Lord led me here." The detailed guidance of God is a literal truth in the individual lives of saints. Our relation to the election of God is the one thing to be concerned over; consequently the need can never be the call. The call is of God, and the engineering of our circumstances is of God, never on the ground of our usefulness. The call of God relates us to the purpose of God.

The purpose of the missionary's creation—"You have made me" (Job 10:9). The first thing God does with us after sanctification is to "force through the channels of a single heart" the interests of the whole world by introducing into us the nature of the Holy Spirit. The nature of the Holy Spirit is the nature of the Son of God; the nature of the Son of God is the nature of Almighty God, and the nature of Almighty God is focused in John 3:16. When we are born from above the realization dawns that we are built for God, not for ourselves. You have made me. We are brought by means of a new birth into the individual realization of God's great purpose for the human race, and all our small, miserable, parochial notions disappear.

If we have been living much in the presence of God the first thing that strikes us is the smallness of the lives of men and women who do not recognize God. It did not occur to us before, their lives seemed to be broad and generous; but now there seems such a fuss of interests that have nothing whatever to do with God's purpose, and are altogether unrelated to the election of God. It is because people live in the things they possess instead of in their relationship to God that God at times seems to be cruel. There are a thousand and one interests that God's providential hand has to brush aside as hopelessly irrelevant to His purpose, and if we have been living in those interests, we go with them (See Luke 12:15).

"The Lord has called Me from the womb" (Isa. 49:1). In this rugged phrase Isaiah declares the creative purpose of God for Israel and Judah. Creation has the opposite meaning to selection. The essential pride of Israel and Judah (and of the Pharisees in our Lord's day) was that God was obliged to select them because of their superiority to other nations. God did not select them: God created them for one purpose, to be His bondslaves.

There were no nations until after the flood. After the flood the human race was split up into nations, and God called off one stream of the human race in Abraham and created a nation out of that one man. (See Gen. 12:2, ff.) The Old Testament is not a history of the nations of the world, but the history of that one nation. In secular history Israel is disregarded as being merely a miserable horde of slaves, and justly so from the standpoint of the historian. The nations to which the Bible pays little attention are much finer to read about, but they have no importance in the redemptive purpose of God. His purpose was the creation of a nation to be His bondslave, that through that nation all the other nations should come to know Him.

The idea that Israel was a magnificently developed type of nation is a mistaken one. Israel was a despised and a despicable nation, continually turning away from God into idolatry; but nothing ever altered the purpose of God for the nation. The despised element is always a noticeable element in the purpose of God. When the Savior of the world came He came of that despised nation; He Himself was "despised and rejected by men" (Isa. 53:3) and in all Christian enterprise there is this same despised element, "things that are despised God has chosen" (1 Cor. 1:28).

The realization by regeneration of the election of God, and of being made thereby perfectly fit for Him, is the most joyful realization on earth. When we are born from above we realize the election of God, our being regenerated does not create it. When we realize that through the salvation of Jesus we are made perfectly fit for God we understand why Jesus is apparently so ruthless in His claims, why He demands such rectitude from saints: He has given us the very nature of God.

The creative purpose of God for the missionary is to make him or her His servant, one in whom He is glorified. When we realize this all our self-conscious limitations will be extinguished in the extraordinary blaze of what redemption means. We have to see that we keep the windows of our souls open to God's creative purpose for us, and not confuse that purpose with our own intentions. Every time we do so, God has to crush our intentions and push them to one side, however it may hurt, because they are on the wrong line. We must beware lest we forget God's purpose for our lives.

The Election of Perfect Finish for God

God elected a certain nation to be His bondslave, and through that nation a knowledge of His salvation is to come to all the world. The history of that nation is a record of awful idolatry and backsliding. They remained true neither to God's prophets nor to God Himself; but in spite of everything the fulfillment of God's purpose for the nation of His choice is certain. The election of the nation by God was not for the salvation of individuals; the elect nation was to be the instrument of salvation to the whole world. The story of their distress is due entirely to their deliberate determination to use themselves for a purpose other than God's The beginning of their corruption was their desire to have a king and to be like other nations. "No, but we will have a king over us, that we also may be like all the nations, and that our king may judge us and go out before us and fight our battles" (1 Sam. 8:19-20). Whenever Israel sought to use themselves for their own purposes, God smashed up those purposes.

We must be careful not to confuse the predestination of God by making His election include every individual, or to have the idea that because God elected a certain nation through whom His salvation was to come, that every individual of that nation is elected to salvation. The history of the elect nation disproves this, but it does not alter God's purpose for the nation. Individuals of the elect nation disprove this, but it does not alter God's purpose for the nation. Individuals of the elect nation have to be saved in the same way as individuals of nations that have not been elected. Election refers to the unchangeable purpose of God, not to the salvation of individuals.

Each individual has to choose which line of predestination to take, God's line or the devil's line. Individual position is determined by individual choice, but that is neither here nor there in connection with God's purpose for the human race. Individuals enter into the realization of the creative purpose of God for the human race by being born again of the Spirit; but we must not make the predestination of God for the race to include every individual, any more than God's predestination for the elect nation included every individual. Salvation is of universal application, but human responsibility is not done away with.

The purpose of God for mankind is that we should "glorify God and enjoy Him for ever" (Westminster Confession of Faith).

Sin has switched the human race off on to another line, but it has not altered God's purpose for the human race in the tiniest degree. The election of the perfect fitness for God of the human race is abiding. It is exhibited in the Man Christ Jesus, and that is the ideal the human race is destined to reach in spite of all that sin and the devil can do—the "measure of the stature of the fullness of Christ" (Eph. 4:13). As Son of Man, Jesus Christ mirrors what the human race is to be like on the basis of redemption. Sin and the devil may do their worst, but God's purpose will only be made manifest all the more gloriously (See Rom. 5:12–21).

Preparation of the missionary's characteristic—"He has made My mouth like a sharp sword" (Isa. 49:2).

The outstanding characteristic of the ancient people of God, of our Lord Jesus Christ, and of the missionary, is the prophetic or preaching characteristic. In the Old Testament the prophet's calling is placed above that of king and of priest. It is the lives of the prophets that prefigure the Lord Jesus Christ. The character of the prophet is essential to his work. The characteristic of God's elective purpose in the finished condition of His servant is that of preaching. "It pleased God by the foolishness of preaching to save them that believe."

Notice the emphasis that the New Testament places on confessing, on preaching, and on testifying, all expressive of this perfect finish for God. And notice too, that it is this characteristic that Satan attacks. He is at the back of the movement abroad today which advocates living a holy life, but "don't talk about it." People never suffer because they live godly lives; they suffer for their speech. Humanly speaking, if our Lord had held His tongue He would not have been put to death. "If I had not come and spoken to them, they would have no sin, but now they have no excuse for their sin" (John 15:22).

A saint is made by God: You made me. Then do not tell God He is a bungling workman. We do that whenever we say "I can't." To say "I can't" literally means we are too strong in ourselves to depend on God. "I can't pray in public; I can't talk in the open air." Substitute "I won't," and it will be nearer the truth. The thing that makes us say "I can't" is that we forget that we must rely entirely on the creative purpose of God and on this characteristic of perfect finish for God.

Much of our difficulty comes because we choose our own work—"Oh well, this is what I am fitted for." Remember that Jesus took a fisherman and turned him into a shepherd. That is symbolic of what He does all the time. Indoor work has to do with civilization; we were created for out-of-door work, both naturally and spiritually. The idea that we have to consecrate our gifts to God is a dangerous one. We cannot consecrate what is not ours (1 Cor. 4:7). We have to consecrate ourselves, and leave our gifts alone. God does not ask us to do the thing that is easy to us naturally; He only asks us to do the thing that we are perfectly fitted to do by grace, and the Cross will always come along that line.

The Election of Perfect Fittedness to God

Israel is still in the shadow of God's hand, in spite of all her wickedness. God's purposes are always fulfilled no matter how wide a compass He may permit to be taken first.

The plan of the missionary's concentration—"In the shadow of His hand He has hidden Me" (Isa. 49:2).

As applied to the saint this phrase refers to the experience of knowing, not with a sigh, but with deepest satisfaction that "In all the world there is none but Thee, my God, there is none but Thee." The shadow of God's hand may seem to be the cruelest, most appalling shadow that ever fell on human life, but we shall find what the disciples found. They feared as they entered the cloud and "suddenly . . . they saw . . . only Jesus with themselves" (Mark 9:8).

Never misunderstand the shadow of God's hand. When He puts us there it is assuredly to lead us into the inner meaning of Phil. 3:10, "That I may know Him." The stern discipline that looks like distress and chastisement turns out to be the biggest benediction; it is the shadow of God's hand that keeps us perfectly fitted in Him.

The kindness and the generosity of God are known when we come under the shadow of His hand. We may kick if we like, or fume, and the fingers hurt; but when we stop kicking, the fingers caress. To say, "Through the shadow of bereavement I came to know God better" is different from saying, "God took away my child because I loved him too much." That is a lie, and contrary to the God of love Jesus revealed. If there is a dark line in God's face to us, the solution does not lie in saying what is not true to fact, but in bowing our heads and waiting; the explanation is not yet. All that is dark and obscure just now will one day be as radiantly and joyously clear as the truth about God we already know. No wonder our Lord's counsel is, "Fear not."

The Missionary Goal

In natural life we have ambitions and aims that alter as we develop; in the Christian life the goal is given at the beginning, our Lord Himself. "Till we all come to the unity of the faith and of the knowledge of the Son of God, to a perfect man, to the measure of the stature of the fullness of Christ" (Eph. 4:13). We do not start with our idea of what the Christian life should be, we start with Christ, and we end with Christ. Our aims in natural life continually alter as we develop but development in the Christian life is an increasing manifestation of Jesus Christ.

Companionship with His Goal

"Behold, we are going up to Jerusalem" (Luke 18:31).

That is not the language of a martyr living beyond His dispensation. Our Lord is not foreseeing with the vision of a highly sensitive nature that His life must end in disaster. He states over and over again that He came on purpose to die. "From that time Jesus began to show to His disciples that He must go to Jerusalem, and suffer many things from the elders and chief priests and scribes, and be killed, and be raised the third day" (Matt. 16:21). The Scriptures leave no room for the idea that our Lord was a martyr (see Luke 24:25–27). Jerusalem stands in the life of our Lord as the place where He reached the climax of His Father's will.

This word of our Lord's is taken as exhibiting the missionary goal, "Behold, we are going up to Jerusalem," and unless we go with Him there, we shall have no companionship with Him. The New Testament centers round one Person, the Lord Jesus Christ. We are regenerated into His kingdom by means of His Cross, and then we go up to our Jerusalem, having His life as our example. We must be born from above before we can go up to our Jerusalem, and the things He met with on His way will throw a flood of light on the things we shall meet. Our Jerusalem means the place where we reach the climax of our Lord's will for us, which is that we may be made one with Him as He is one with the Father. The aim of the missionary is not to win the unbelieving, nor to be useful, but to do God's will. Missionaries do win the unbelieving, and they are useful, but that is not their aim; their aim is to do the will of their Lord.

Considering His Facing of the Way

"He steadfastly set His face to go to Jerusalem" (Luke 9:51).

The set purpose of our Lord's life was to do the will of His Father; that was His dominating interest all through. He went on His way to Jerusalem unhasting and unresting, not hurrying through the villages where they did not receive Him because His face was as though He were going to Jerusalem, nor loitering in those villages where they welcomed Him. Our danger is to be deflected by the things we meet with on the way to our Jerusalem. "I am so misunderstood and so persecuted here that I must get away," or, "This is where I am so useful that I must stay awhile."

Ambition means a set purpose for the attainment of our own ideals, and as such it is excluded from the kingdom of our Lord. When the disciples asked "Who then is greatest in the kingdom of heaven?" Jesus called to Him a little child and said,

"Unless you . . . become as little children, you will by no means enter the kingdom of heaven" (Matt. 18:1–3). The nature of the kingdom of heaven is revealed in the implicit nature of a child, because a child does not work according to a set ambition, but obeys the simple law of childish nature. If we are children of God the simple law of our nature is the Holy Spirit; His one set purpose is the glorification of Jesus, and He pays no attention to our secular or our religious notions.

Are we entering into competition with the purpose of the Holy Spirit by having purposes and ambitions of our own? As we face the way to our Jerusalem, we must adhere to the set purpose of the Holy Spirit, which is to glorify Jesus. We must never be deflected by the pride of those who reject us because of that purpose, nor be deterred by the prejudices of those in the same way with us. We must consider Him, and go up to Jerusalem with Him. The "one thing" in the life of the apostle Paul was not an ambition; it was a set purpose born of the Holy Spirit in him.

Comparing His Faring on the Way

"And He went through the cities and villages, teaching, and journeying toward Jerusalem" (Luke 13:22).

Our Lord was not fanatical. Had He been a fanatic, He would have said, "Because I am going up to Jerusalem there is no need to stay in this village or that; I have only one duty, and that is to go up to Jerusalem." Our Lord took plenty of time to do His duty in the cities and villages that He went through on His way up to Jerusalem. Nothing made Him hurry through the villages where He was persecuted, or linger in those where He was blessed.

Our Lord met deceit on His way to Jerusalem, but it did not deter Him from His set purpose (see Luke 13:31–33).

Our Lord also realized desperate distress on His way, but nothing caused Him to swerve one hair's breadth from the set purpose of God (see Luke 13:34–35).

As workers for God we shall meet with deceit and with distress on the way to Jerusalem, for "the disciple is not above his teacher" (Matt. 10:24). It is true of the Master that "He will not fail nor be discouraged" (Isa. 42:4). In the intimate circle of our Lord's own disciples there was one whom He called a devil, but He never allowed that to deter or discourage Him.

Various things will make us forget to do our duty, like excess of joy (see Acts 12:12). In the excitement of a revival we become so taken up with joy that we forget the home duties and everything else.

Contemplating His Findings on the Way

"Now it happened as He went to Jerusalem . . . there met Him ten men who were lepers" (Luke 17:11–19).

Our Lord met ingratitude on His way to Jerusalem—"Were there not ten cleansed? But where are the nine?"—but it did not turn Him from His purpose. We will meet the same thing on the way to our Jerusalem; there will be people who get blessed and one or two will show gratitude, and the rest, gross ingratitude. Never allow this feeling to come in—"Well, I am going to do no more for that one, I did everything I could and all I got was gross ingratitude." That sentiment will deflect us from going up to our Jerusalem. We are not here to serve our own purposes; we are here, by the grace of God and by His indwelling Spirit, to glorify our Lord and Master. If He brings us up against callous people, mean, ungrateful, sponging people, we must never turn our faces for one second from our Jerusalem, because that is a temper of mind in which Jesus cannot be glorified.

We have to learn to go the second mile with God. Some of us get played out in the first ten yards because God compels us to go where we cannot see the way, and we think we will wait until we get nearer the big crisis. We can all see the big crisis, "Oh yes I would like to do that for God," but what about the obscure duty waiting to be done? If we do not do the walking, steadily and carefully, in the little matters, we will do nothing when the big crisis comes. We shall flag when there is no vision, no uplift—just the common round, the trivial task; but if we keep our faces steadfastly set towards our Jerusalem and go there considering Him, it will not be possible for drudgery to damp us.

Concerning His Finishing on the Way—"He spoke another parable, because He was near Jerusalem" (Luke 19:11).

As our Lord drew near to His cross the disciples became more and more perplexed, until at last, at the end of three years of the most intimate contact with Him, they said "What is this that He says? . . . We do not know what He is saying" (John 16:18). After the Resurrection our Lord breathed on them and said, "Receive the Holy Spirit" (John 20:22). "Then their eyes were opened, and they knew Him" (Luke 24:31). "Then He opened their understanding, that they might comprehend the Scriptures" (Luke 24:45). If we try to get "head first" into what our Lord teaches, we shall exhibit the same stupidity as the disciples did until we have received the Holy Spirit and learned to rely on Him, and to interpret the words of Jesus as He brings them to our minds.

Consummating His Fulfillment at the Goal

"There they crucified Him." (Luke 23:33).

That is what happened to our Lord when He reached Jerusalem, but that event is the gateway to our salvation. By His death on the Cross our Lord made the way for every human being to come into communion with God. The saints do not end in crucifixion; by the Lord's grace, we end in glory. In the meantime the missionary's watchword is—"Behold I, too, go up to Jerusalem."

The Missionary Problem

Scheme of Enterprise

"Ask of Me, and I will give You the nations for Your inheritance, and the ends of the earth for Your possession" (Ps. 2:8).

The emphasis in this psalm and all through the Bible is that missionary enterprise is God's thought, not man's. We do not know apart from the Spirit of God what God's purpose is. The problems surrounding work in the mission field, and any branch of Christian work, are too big to cope with by man's intellect alone; yet the humblest saint in communion with God works out God's answer to every problem, for the most part unconsciously to himself. To attempt to understand the problems that are pressing on the shores of Christian work today at home and abroad, apart from God, will result in an absolute bewilderment of mind and spirit. It must all come back to one point, a personal relationship to God in Christ Jesus.

There is nothing simple in the human soul or in human life; only one thing is simple, and that is the relationship of the individual soul to God, "the simplicity that is in Christ" (2 Cor. 11:3). In work for God it is not sufficient to be awake to the need, to be in earnest, to want to do something; it is necessary to prove from every standpoint, moral, intellectual, and spiritual, that the only way to live is in personal relationship to God. It is the individual men and women living lives rooted and grounded in God who are fulfilling God's purpose in the world.

The great Author and Originator of all missionary enterprise is God and we must keep in touch with His line. The call to the missionary does not arise out of the discernment of our own minds, nor from the sympathy of our own hearts, but because behind the face of every distorted, downtrodden unbeliever we see the face of Jesus Christ and hear His command, "Go therefore and make disciples of all the nations" (Matt. 28:19). The need of the unbelieving world can only be met by our risen Lord who has all power in heaven and in earth, and by our receiving from Him the endowment of power from on high. We have to see that we conserve the energy of regenerating grace planted in us by the Holy Spirit through the Atonement, then wherever we go the rivers of living water will flow through our lives.

From the very beginning God's work has seemed a forlorn hope, as if He were being worsted; all the arguments seem to be in favor of working on other lines—the line of education, of healing, and of civilization. These are the "birds" that come and lodge in the branches, and some are saying that the present manifestation of civilization is the outcome of Christianity. "This," they say, "is Christianity, this is the real thing, these educational forces, these healing and civilizing forces. This is what missions ought to be doing, not going off on the line of personal sanctification or of devotion to Jesus; we have grown out of all that. We must devote ourselves to the things we can see; we must educate and train these benighted races and introduce our wider, better views, and in that way the kingdom of God will come in." This is not God's way.

God will bring in His kingdom in His own way. Jesus says that in this dispensation "the kingdom of God is within you" (Luke 17:21). All these forces of civilization have been allowed to lodge in the branches of the spiritual tree of Christianity while the Life that makes them possible is not recognized. They receive shelter from that which they are not themselves and their eyes are blind to the real issue. It is astounding how far away people will get when they leave the humble stand of lives hid with Christ in God.

Spiritual Evangelization

" 'And the nations shall know that I am the Lord,' says the Lord God, 'when I am hallowed in you before their eyes' " (Ezek. 36:23).

The first purpose of missionary enterprise is evangelistic, and the evangel is that of personal sanctification. A missionary and a Christian ought to be one and the same, and a Christian is one who is united to the Lord by a living union of character. It is easy to rouse enthusiasm along medical, educational and industrial lines, on the ground that wherever Christianity is made known social development follows. This is true, but all these things are secondary. The first aim of missionary enterprise is the spiritual evangelization of the people, and the missionary must be united to Jesus Christ by the spiritual bond of sanctification before he or she can evangelize others.

Wherever Christians are placed, we must work out the sanctified life. We have to beware of the notion that spirituality is something divorced from contact with sordid realities. The one and only test of a spiritual life is in practical reality. When a missionary's life is taken and placed down under the black night of unbelief there is only one thing that can stand, and that is the sanctification wrought by God—a personal union with Jesus Christ, and the realization that we are here for one purpose only, to make disciples of Jesus Christ.

If missionary enthusiasm is awakened without missionary knowledge being given, men and women go out totally unprepared to face the conditions in foreign lands. And every hour of the day they are faced with moral problems that shock every human sensibility. Unless the call of God has been heard, and the mind and nerves are prepared to face these things from God's standpoint, the whole nature fails under the strain and the result is either that the missionary returns home broken or sinks down into oblivion on the mission field itself. We have to call ourselves up short in reading missionary books that sweep us off our feet and see if they tally with God's purpose. It is extraordinary how few of them do. It is the needs of the unbelieving that are put first, the awfulness of the conditions that prevail in foreign lands.

None of this constitutes the call for a missionary. The appeal is based on the command of our Lord, "Go therefore and make disciples of all the nations" (Matt. 28:19), not, go because the conditions of the unbelieving will be improved. They will be, but the great motive of the missionary is the command of Jesus Christ for spiritual evangelization. We have to guard our motives in work for God as jealously as we would guard anything that God actually puts into our hands. It needs more courage to face God with our motives in work for Him than it does to face an audience with our message. We have continually to face our own personal sanctification and our motives for service with the Lord Himself, to let His searchlight come, and to see that we remain true to Him. We are not sent to develop the races, we are sent to preach the Gospel to every creature because our Lord has commanded it, and for no other reason. God's purpose is at the back of the whole thing, and His purpose is revealed by His Spirit to sanctified souls only.

Today people are trying to better Jesus Christ's program and are saying that they must first of all look after human bodies, heal them and teach them, and then evangelize them. This reminds one of the legend which says that the birds decided that whichever of them could fly the highest would be their king; whereupon the wren perched on the back of the eagle, and when the eagle soared up into the sky, the little wren flew up higher still. Many modern writers on missionary enterprise are like the wren on the back of the eagle: they think they can go one better than Jesus Christ. His teaching was all very well for the beginning stages, but now we can go one better.

Missionary enterprise on the line of education, and healing, and social amelioration is magnificent, but it is secondary, and the danger is to give it the first place. The temptation is more subtle today than ever it has been because the countries of the world are being opened up as never before. It sounds so plausible and right to say heal the people, teach them, put them in better surroundings, and then evangelize them; but it is fundamentally wrong. The cry, "Civilize first and then evangelize," has honeycombed itself into missionary work in every land; and it takes the Spirit of God to show where it is in direct opposition to God's line. It is putting human needs first, and that is the very heart and kernel of the temptation Satan brought to our Lord.

Our Lord's first obedience was not to the needs of human beings, but to the will of His Father. We must beware of putting anything first that Jesus does not put first. The testimony of missionaries over and over again is to the effect that when once evangelistic work is put in the second place, it is the devil who gets his way, not God. Dr. Moffatt said that civilization drives away the tiger, but breeds the fox. That was the statement of a man after years of work in the mission field, and with ample opportunity of estimating all the forces at work. The introduction of civilization, without the emphasis on living the life hid with Christ in God, tends to increase the power of evil because it covers it with a veil of refinement.

"The nations shall know that I am the Lord . . . when I am hallowed in you before their eyes." The only reason for a Christian to go out to the mission field is that his or her own life is hid with Christ in God. The compulsion of the providence of

God outside, working with the imperative call of His Spirit inside, has wedded itself to the command of Jesus, "Go therefore and make disciples of all the nations." The awakening force spiritually will not come from the civilization of the West, but from the lives of the lonely, obscure missionaries who have stood true to God and through whom the rivers of living water have flowed.

Supernatural Hope for Missions

"Thus says the Lord: 'Stand in the ways and see, and ask for the old paths, where the good way is, and walk in it; and you will find rest for your souls' " (Jer. 6:16).

In looking back over centuries of missionary work the tendency is to say, "This is where that effort failed, and this is where the other failed," but the real reason for the failure is missed: that God's ideal had been abandoned. If you talk about the need for personal sanctification to aggressive Christian workers they will say, "You are a dreamer of dreams, we have to get to work and do something." It is not a question of doing things, but a question of realizing deep down until there is no shadow of doubt about it that if we are going to do anything it must be by the supernatural power of God, not by our own ingenuity and wisdom.

Holiness people are not impractical, they are the only ones who are building on the great underlying ideal of God. Our business as workers for God is to find out what God's ideal is, to ask ourselves on what line we are doing our duty: whether we are progressing along the line of God's ideal, and working that out, or being caught up in the drift of modern views and evolving away from God's ideal. The Sermon on the Mount is the perpetual standard of measurement for those at work for God, and yet the statements of Jesus Christ are continually being watered down and even contradicted by many today. There is not the slightest use in going to the foreign field to work for God if we are not true to His ideal at home. We would be a disgrace to Him there.

How many of us really live up to all the light we have? If we examine ourselves before God, we will find that we dare not go one step beyond our own crowd no matter what the Lord says. If we get any new light on God's Word, or on His will for our lives, we take on the cringe of the coward: "I wonder if the others have seen that," or, "Oh well, if they do not do it, I must not." Very few of us walk up to the light we get unless someone else will go with us.

For instance, if we notice how often Jesus Christ talks about being persecuted and cast out for His name's sake, we shall soon see how far we have fallen away from His ideal. Even the most spiritual among us have little of the genius of the Holy Spirit in our lives. We accept the ordinary, common sense ways of doing things without ever examining them in the light of God. When we do begin to re-relate our lives in accordance with God's ideal we will encounter the scorn, or the amazement, or the ridicule, or pity of the crowd we belong to.

There are books and teachers that tell us that when God is at work in our lives it will be manifested in ostensible ways of blessing. Jesus says that the ostensible way in which it will work out is the way of ridicule. "As He is, so are we in this world" (1 John 4:17). What we are insisting on is a right relationship to God first and then the carrying out of work along God's line. Whether our work is a success or a failure has nothing to do with us. Our call is not to successful service but to faithfulness.

Our Lord demands of us a personal, watchful relationship to Himself and the doing of the duty that lies nearest from that standpoint. Whether others recognize it or not, it will tell for eternity whether we are in the home or the foreign field. It depends on our standpoint which line we emphasize: a personal relationship to Jesus Christ first, then from that basis as much practical work as possible. Unless the missionary is based on a right relationship to God, he or she will fizzle out in the passing of the years and become a negligible quantity from God's standpoint. The men and women who stand absolutely true to God's ideal are the ones who are telling for God. God has staked His honor on the work of Jesus Christ in the souls of those whom He has saved, and sanctified, and sent.

The Key to the
Missionary Problem

Matthew 9:38

The Key to the Master's Orders

"Therefore pray . . ."

The key to the missionary problem is in the hands of God, not of humanity, and according to our Lord the key is prayer, not work, as that word is popularly understood, because work may mean evading spiritual concentration. Our Lord said, "Therefore pray."

We are not speaking of the lock which the key has to open, the problems of missionary enterprise, but of the key to those problems. That key is put into our hands by Jesus Christ, and it is not a commonsense key. It is not a medical key, nor a civilizing key, nor an educational key, not even an evangelical key; the key is prayer. We are challenged straight away by the difference between our view of prayer and our Lord's view. Prayer to us is not practical, it is stupid, and until we do see that prayer is stupid, stupid from the ordinary, natural, common sense point of view, we will never pray. It is absurd to think that God is going to alter things in answer to prayer. But that is what Jesus says He will do. It sounds stupid, but it is a stupidity based on His redemption. The reason that our prayers are not answered is that we are not stupid enough to believe what Jesus says. It is a child, and only a child who has prayer answered; a wise and prudent adult does not (see Matthew 11:25). We have to be as natural as children in our relationship to Jesus Christ and He does His work all the time. Jesus Christ is our Master and He lays down His orders very distinctly, "Therefore pray."

Prayer the work—John 14:12–14. We are apt to think of prayer as a commonsense exercise of our higher powers in order to prepare us for work, whereas in the teaching of Jesus prayer is not to fit us for the "greater works," prayer is the work. Prayer is the outcome of our apprehension of the nature of God, the means whereby we assimilate more and more of His mind, and the means whereby He unveils His purposes to us.

Prayer the fruit—John 15:16. The way fruit remains is by prayer. Our Lord puts prayer as the means to fruit-producing and fruit-abiding work; but remember it is prayer based on His agony, not on our agony. God is not impressed by our earnestness; He nowhere promises to answer prayer because of our agony in intercession, but only on the ground of redemption. We have "boldness to enter the Holiest by the blood of Jesus" (Heb. 10:19), and in no other way. We take the crown off redemption as the ground on which God answers prayer and put it on our own earnestness. Prayer is the miracle of redemption at work in us, which will produce the miracle of redemption in the lives of others.

Prayer the battle—Eph. 6:11–20.

The armor is for the battle of prayer. "Put on the whole armor of God. . . . Stand therefore," and then pray.

The armor is not to fight in, but to shield us while we pray. Prayer is the battle. The reason we do not pray is that we do not own Jesus Christ as Master, we do not take our orders from Him. The key to the Master's orders is prayer, and where we are when we pray is a matter of absolute indifference. In whatever way God is engineering our circumstances, that is the duty—to pray.

The Key to the Master's Ownership
"the Lord of the harvest . . ."

According to our Lord He owns the harvest, and the harvest is the crisis in innumerable lives all over the world. "Therefore pray the Lord of the harvest," not pray because we are wrought up over the needs of the unbelievers, nor pray to procure funds for a society, but pray to the Lord of the harvest. It is appalling how little attention we pay to what our Lord says.

"As the Father has sent Me, I also send you" (John 20:21)—to put in a sickle, to reap. All over the world there are crises in lives; they are all around us, unbelieving and Christian. We meet them by the score every day we live, but unless we are set on obeying our Master's orders we shall never see them. Supposing the crisis comes in my father's life, my brother's life, am I there as a laborer that the harvest may be reaped for Jesus? Jesus said, "Go therefore and make disciples of all the nations"; and we cannot disciple others unless we ourselves are disciples. The evangelical emphasis has too often been, "So many souls saved, thank God, now they are all right," the idea being that we have done this thing for God. It is God who saves; we have to do the discipling after people are saved.

His position in His own world—Col. 1:16–18. Our Lord's position in His own world is that of Creator. From the remotest star to the last grain of sand, "By Him all things were created" (Col. 1:16). His own creatures always recognized Him—"He came unto His own things" (John 1:11, RSV marg.). They do not recognize our lordship because we have too much of the brute about us; the whole "creation eagerly waits for the revealing of the sons of God" (Rom. 8:19).

His position among His own people—John 1:11. "And His own did not receive Him." Jesus is never recognized by anyone until the personal crisis of conviction of sin is reached. He is the owner of the harvest, not of everyone; they will not have Him until this point of crisis is reached. Jesus Christ owns the harvest which is produced in individuals by the distress of conviction of sin; and it is this harvest we have to pray that laborers may be thrust out to reap. We may be taken up with the activities of a denomination, or be giving ourselves up to this committee and that, while all about us people are ripe for harvest and we do not reap one of them, but waste our Lord's time in over-energized activities for furthering some cause or denomination.

Jesus Christ is the Lord of the harvest. There are no nations whatever in His outlook, no respect of persons with Him; His outlook is the world. How many of us pray without respect of persons, and with respect to one person only, Jesus Christ?

His position over His own disciples—John 17:6. "They were Yours, You gave them to Me." The disciple is Christ's own, and the disciple is not above the Master. He tells us to pray, His Spirit is abroad, and the fields are ready to harvest, but the eyes of all saving His disciples are blind. If for one whole day, quietly and determinedly, we were to give ourselves up to the ownership of Jesus and to obeying His orders, we should be amazed at its close to realize all He had packed into that one day. We say, "Oh, but I have special work to do." Every Christian is called to be Jesus Christ's own, one chosen by Him; one who is not above the Master, and who does not dictate to Jesus as to what he or she intends to do. Our Lord calls to no special work; He calls to Himself. Pray to the Lord of the harvest, and He will engineer your circumstances and thrust you out.

The Key to the Master's Option
". . . to send out laborers into His harvest."

The form the prayer is to take is also dictated by the Master: "to send out laborers into His harvest." This leaves no room for the "amateur providence" notion which arises out of our neglect to take our orders from Jesus Christ. We must pray to the Lord of the harvest and take our orders from Him and from no one else. The desire to be an amateur providence always arises when Jesus Christ is not recognized as the universal Sovereign.

The direction of the work—John 4:35–38. The others who labored are the prophets and apostles, "and you have entered into their labors" (v. 38). The great Sower of the seed of redemption is the Holy Spirit. The direction of the work is at the option of the Master, not at the choice of the disciple. Mark the significance of the term labor. We refuse to pray unless we get thrills. May God save us from that counterfeit of true prayer, it is the most intense form of spiritual selfishness. We have to labor, and to labor along the line of His direction. Jesus Christ says, Pray. It looks stupid; but when we labor at prayer results happen all the time from His standpoint, because God creates something in answer to and by means of prayer that was not in existence before. Labor. It is the one thing we will not do. We will take open-air meetings, we will preach—but labor at prayer! There is nothing thrilling about a laborer's work, but it is the laborer who makes the conceptions of the genius possible; and it is the laboring saint who makes the conceptions of our Master possible.

The disposition of the worker—Matthew 10:24. Wherever the providence of God may dump us down—in a slum, in a shop, in the desert—we have to labor along the line of His direction. Never allow this thought, "I am of no use where I am," because you certainly can be of no use where you are not! Wherever He has engineered your circumstances, pray to Him all the time. Impulsive prayer, the prayer that looks so futile, is the thing God heeds more than anything else. Jesus says, "If you abide in Me, and My words abide in you, you will ask what you desire, and it shall be done for you" (John 15:7).

Think what an astonishment it will be when the veil is lifted to find the number of souls that have been reaped for Jesus because our disposition has made Him Master and we are in the habit of taking our orders from Him. Our Lord in one of His parables reveals that God sows His saints in the places that are most useless according to the judgment of the world; He puts them where He likes. Where God is being glorified is where He puts His saints, and we are no judge of where that is.

The distinctness of the way—John 14:6. The Master says He is the Way; then abide in Him. He says He is the Truth; then believe in Him. He says He is the Life; then live in Him.

Prayer is the answer to every problem there is. How else could our Lord's command in John 14:1 be fulfilled in our experience? How could we have an untroubled heart if we believed that the unbelievers who have not heard the gospel are damned? What would redemption of Jesus Christ be worth, of what use would the revelation given in John 3:16 be, if it depended on the laggard laziness of Christians as to whether people are to be saved or not?

We have to live depending on Jesus Christ's wisdom, not on our own. He is the Master, and the problem is His, not ours. We have to use the key He gives us, the key of prayer. Our Lord puts the key into our hands and we have to learn to pray under His direction. That is the simplicity which He says His Father will bless.

The Key to the Missionary

Matthew 28:16–20

The Universal Sovereignty of Christ

"All authority has been given to Me in heaven and on earth" (v. 18).

The "all things" of Matt. 11:27 is limited to the revelation of the Father; the "all authority" of Matt. 28:18 refers to the absolute, sovereign, universal power of the risen Lord. "All authority has been given to Me. . . . Go therefore, and make disciples of all the nations." The basis of the missionary appeal is the authority of Jesus Christ.

Our Lord puts Himself as the supreme sovereign Lord over His disciples. He does not say the unbelieving will be lost if you do not go, but simply, "This is My commandment to you as My disciples"—"Go and make disciples of all the nations." Jesus did not say go into all the world or go into the foreign field, but simply, "Go and make disciples," that is, "preach and teach out of a living experience of Myself." We are all based on a conception of importance, either our own importance or the importance of someone else; Jesus tells us to go and teach based on the revelation of His importance. "All authority has been given to Me. . . . Go therefore."

The real solitude with Christ—"Then the eleven disciples went away into Galilee, to the mountain . . ." (v. 16).

The disciples had been in intimate fellowship with Jesus day and night for three years; they had seen Him go through the unfathomable agony of Gethsemane; they had seen Him put to death on Calvary; they had seen Him after His resurrection, and now they stand in solitude with Him. If we want to know the universal sovereignty of Christ we must get into solitude with Him. It is not sufficient for someone else to tell us about Him; we must perceive with our own eyes who He is, we must know Him for ourselves. Jesus Christ alone is the key to the missionary.

The danger today is to make practical work the driving wheel of our enterprises for God. All the intense social work and aggressive movements of our day are apt to be anti-Christian. They are antagonistic to the sovereignty of the Lord Jesus Christ because they are based on the conception that human ingenuity is going to bring in the kingdom of God, and Jesus Christ is made of no account.

The right spot to meet Christ—". . . which Jesus had appointed for them."

"Come to Me, all you who labor and are heavy laden" (Matt. 11:28), and how many missionaries are! We banish these marvelous words of the universal Sovereign of the world to the threshold of an evangelistic after-meeting. They are the words of Jesus to His disciples. He says Come, and we have deliberately to take time to come. If we do not take time to come, we shall be inclined to call God's messages the devil. We are so busy in work for Him that when He just touches us, down we go, and in our panic we say, "Oh! that must be the devil." It was God. "Do not despise the chastening of the Lord" (Heb. 12:5).

We must get to the place of real solitude with Christ. He is our mountain-height and our sea-calm. He is the recreating power; He is the universal Sovereign. He tells us to consider the lilies; we say, "No, we must consider life." We mistake the mechanism of life for life itself, and that idea has become incorporated into Christian work. In the active work we do for God we do not really believe that Jesus Christ is sovereign Lord;

if we did, we would fuss less and build more in faith in Him. We cannot do the Savior's work by fuss, but only by knowing Him as the supreme, sovereign Lord.

The rectified sight of Christ—"When they saw Him, they worshipped Him; but some doubted" (Matt. 28:17).

It is not the doubt of unbelief but the doubt of wonder: "Can it really be so simple as that?" If it is not as simple as that it is all wrong. When we transacted business with the sovereign Christ, the misgiving in our hearts was that it was too simple. The simplicity is the very thing that is of Jesus; anything that is not simple is not of Him. Anything that is complicated is not of His sovereignty but of our self-interest, our self-will, our self-consideration.

It is a great thing to have our spiritual sight tested by the Celestial Optician, to watch the way in which He rectifies and readjusts our sight. There is one unmistakable witness that Jesus promised us, and that is the gift of His peace. "My peace I give to you" (John 14:27). No matter how complicated the circumstances may be, one moment of contact with Jesus and the fuss is gone, the panic is gone, all the shallow emptiness is gone, and His peace is put in; absolute tranquillity, because of what He says, "All authority has been given to Me." Do we look and act as if we believed He has all power in heaven and in earth? What is our actual life like? Is it conducted on the line of John 14:1—an undisturbedness of heart arising out of belief in Jesus? We must remember to take time to worship the Being whose name we bear.

The Unobtrusive Service of the Commission
"Go therefore" (Matt. 28:19)

These words are simply the introduction to a commission. The unobtrusive service of the commission is outlined in the quiet, almost commonplace statement, "Go your way, remembering what I have told you."

How to go—Acts 1:8 There is always the danger of starting up false enthusiasm in missionary work. "Oh yes, I will go; where shall I go?" That is like making a false start in a race and having to go back to the starting point. Our Lord's word go simply means live, and Acts 1:8 describes the going. Jesus did not say to the disciples, go to Jerusalem, go to Judea, go to Samaria, go to the end of the earth, but "You shall be witnesses to Me" in all these places. He undertakes to establish the goings. So many people are obsessed with this idea, "What are you going to do?" I hope none of us are going to do anything; I hope we are going to be what He wants us to be.

In Matthew 28:19, our Lord does not say go into all the world, but "Go therefore and make disciples." He does the engineering. In Acts 1:8, He does not say you shall receive power, and you shall go into Jerusalem, but "You shall be witnesses to Me." How the disciples went is described later in the Acts of the Apostles. They went at the point of the sword; persecution arose and scattered them by the providence of God. How to go refers to the personal spiritual character of the missionary, not to the feet of the missionary.

How to keep going—John 15:7. These wonderful words tell us how to keep going in our personal lives: by the words of Jesus. "If you abide in Me, and My words abide in you." We have to continually pull ourselves up short and recognize the amazing simplicity of Jesus Christ's counsel. The reason we get perplexed is that we do not believe He is sovereign Lord; we do not believe that He will never forget anything we remember; we conjure up a hundred and one things that we imagine He has forgotten.

Instead of praying to the Lord of the harvest to thrust out laborers, we pray, "O Lord, keep my body right; see after this matter and that for me." Our prayers are taken up with our concerns, our own needs, and only once in a while do we pray for what He tells us to. "You will ask what you desire, and it shall be done for you." We must feed on His Word, and that will keep our spiritual lives going. Where we are placed is a matter of indifference. God does the engineering, and He sends us out. "Has God given you a special call to this place?" He never does. The place is arranged for by His providence, not by His call.

How to keep going till we're gone—Acts 20:24.

This verse tells us how to keep going till we're gone: firstly, by allowing no afflictions to move us from our confidence in the sovereignty of Jesus Christ; secondly, by not considering our lives dear to ourselves but only to Jesus Christ for the carrying out of His purposes; and thirdly, by fulfilling the ministry we have received of Him to testify the gospel of the grace of God. Then we shall go all together, like Oliver Wendell Holmes' pony chaise, every part worn out at the same time. That is what happens with a wholesome Christian life.

The Unique Sacrament of the Charter
"And make disciples of all the nations" (Matt. 28:19).

This is the central point of the commission: teach, make disciples of all the nations, disciple everyone, not proselytize everyone. There is nothing more objectionable than a spiritual prig. The type for the missionary is God's own Son, and He did not go about buttonholing people. There were plenty of promising individuals in our Lord's day. One of them came to Jesus and asked what he might do to inherit eternal life, and the words Jesus spoke to him sent him away in heartbreaking discouragement.

Our Lord never pleaded, He never cajoled, He never entrapped; He simply spoke the sternest words mortal ears ever heard, and then left it alone. Our Lord has a perfect understanding that when His word is heard it will bear fruit sooner or later.

Today a number of hysterical and sentimental things are apt to gather round the missionary appeal. The need of the unbelieving is made the basis of the appeal instead of the authority of Jesus Christ. The need is made the call. It may be good up to a certain point, but it is not the line for the disciples of Jesus Christ. Our Lord did not tell His disciples to gather together and select certain people and send them out.

That is what is being done in many places today because we do not take our conception of missionary enterprise from the New Testament. We adapt the New Testament to suit our own ideas; consequently we look on Jesus Christ as one who assists us in our enterprises. The New Testament idea is that Jesus Christ is the absolute Lord over His disciples.

Administer your learning—John 17:17–18. A disciple must administer to those who are ripe for what he or she personally has learned. Jesus Christ is the Lord of the harvest; and the harvest is the critical moment in individual lives that is produced by conviction of sin, and Jesus alone is the judge of when that moment comes.

Many years ago I knew a godly old shepherd in the highlands, John Cameron. He was so marvelously used by God in his contact with people that whenever he talked to them about their souls they would get saved. One summer John said to me, "If you get permission to talk to my plowman about his soul, do."

Naturally, I said, "Why don't you talk to him yourself?"

He replied, "Didn't I say, 'If you get permission'? If you don't know about getting permission, you don't know anything about the Holy Spirit. Do you think I talk to everyone I meet? If I did, I would make God a liar. No, I have to get permission before I talk to a soul."

This plowman was with John for three years, and they were together every day bringing the sheep over the hills and John never once spoke to him about his soul. They would meet people on the hills and John would talk to them and they would get saved. But he never said a word to the plowman about spiritual things, until at last one day the plowman burst out, "For God's sake, talk to me about my soul, or I'll be in hell." So John did talk to him, and the man was wonderfully saved.

Then he asked John Cameron why he had not spoken to him before. And John said, "Probably you know why better than I do—I didn't get permission."

Then the plowman told him this: "When you fed me, I knew you were a religious man, and I said to some of my mates—'If old John talks to me about my soul, I'll let him know what he is doing.' "

So the administering of the Word is not ministering it where we think it is needed; the Word has to be sown in living touch with the Lord of the harvest, sown in touch with Him in solitude and prayer, and He will bring the people round—black and white, educated and uneducated, rich and poor. They are all there, "ready to harvest," but most of us are so keen on our own notions that we do not recognize that they are ripe for reaping. If we are in touch with Jesus Christ, He says all the time, "This is the moment; this one here, that one there, is ready to be reaped."

We say, "Oh, but I want to go and get scores of unbelievers saved, I do not want to be the means of reaping my brother," but your brother happens to be the one who is ready to harvest. The commission is to teach, to disciple, to administer the Word.

Abandon your life—John 20:23.   These words refer to the sacrament of an abandoned life filled with the Holy Spirit, through Whom the sovereign Lord makes His words to be spirit and life. "That was exactly the word I needed; how did you know?" You did not know anything about it, you were living in abandoned devotion to Jesus, and He administered the word through you. It is not done by our wits and ingenuity, by our agony and distress, or by our piety, but entirely by our abandon to Jesus Christ.

Apply your loyalty—Rev. 2:10. These words reveal how to apply our loyalty to our sovereign Lord in every condition and every circumstance: "Be faithful until death."

The key to the missionary is the absolute sovereignty of the Lord Jesus Christ. We must get into real solitude with Him, feed our souls on His Word, and He will engineer our circumstances. "Consider the lilies of the field, how they grow" (Matt. 6:28). They live where they are put, and we have to live where God places us. It is not the going of the feet but the going of the life in real, vital relationship to Jesus Christ. God will bring round a stationary life far more than He can ever bring round a "going" missionary, if the going missionary is not one whose life is hid with Christ in God. The goings must be of God. There are a hundred and one things in human life that we cannot control. But Jesus says, "All authority has been given to Me in heaven and on earth." Then what are we up to with all our worrying? He says, "Let not your heart be troubled . . . believe also in Me" (John 14:1).

"All authority has been given to Me. . . . Go therefore." "Go established in Me, and disciple everyone whom I bring around you; I will tell you when they are ripe for it." We shall find that it is not possible to be self-conscious servants of Jesus. We are never of any use to Him in our self-conscious moments; it is in the ordinary times when we are living simply in faith in Him that He gives out the sacrament of His Word through us. "He who believes in Me . . . out of his heart will flow rivers of living water" (John 7:38).

The Key to the Missionary Message
Luke 24:47–49

The Remissionary Message of the Missionary

"That repentance and remission of sins should be preached in His name . . ." (v. 47).

It is easy to forget that the first duty of the missionary is not to uplift the unbelieving, not to heal the sick, not to civilize savage races, because all that sounds so rational and so human. It is easy to arouse interest in it and get funds for it. The primary duty of the missionary is to preach repentance and remission of sins in His name. The key to the missionary message, whether the missionary is a doctor, a teacher, an industrial worker, or a nurse, is the remissionary purpose of our Lord Jesus Christ's death. The idea of the missionary class, the ministerial class, the Christian worker class has arisen out of our ideas of civilized life, not out of the New Testament faith and order. The New Testament faith and order is that as Christians we do not cease to do our duty as ordinary human beings, but in addition we have been given the key to the missionary message: the proclaiming of the remissionary purpose of the life and death of our Lord. The other work is to be done so instinctively and naturally that it does not interfere with proclaiming the missionary message. We need to remember that Christians must do all that human beings ought to do, and much more, because they are supernaturally endowed, but we must never confound that with what our Lord has entrusted His servants to do, to go and make disciples.

The limitless significance of Christ the Lamb of God—1 John 2:2. It is possible to take any phase of our Lord's life, the healing phase, the

129

teaching phase, the saving and sanctifying phase, but there is nothing limitless about any of these. But take this: "the Lamb of God who takes away the sin of the world" (John 1:29). That is limitless. The key to the missionary message is the limitless significance of Jesus as the propitiation for our sins. A missionary is one who is soaked in the revelation that Jesus Christ is "the propitiation for our sins, and not for ours only but also for the whole world" (1 John 2:2). The key to the missionary message is not the kindness of Jesus; not His going about doing good; not His revealing of the Fatherhood of God; but the remissionary aspect of His life and death. This aspect alone has a limitless significance.

The limitless significance of sin against the Lamb of God—2 Cor. 5:21. If the significance of Christ as the propitiation for sins is limitless, the domain to which His propitiation applies is limitless also. Sinfulness against Christ is as limitless as the propitiation. "Therefore, just as through one man sin entered the world, and death through sin, and thus death spread to all men, because all sinned" (Rom. 5:12). We are apt to talk sentimental nonsense about the universal Fatherhood of God; to knock the bottom board out of redemption by saying that God is love and of course He will forgive sin. When the Holy Spirit comes He makes us know that God is holy love, and therefore He cannot forgive sin apart from the Atonement; He would contradict His own nature if He did. The only ground on which God can forgive sin and reinstate us in His favor is through the Cross of Christ, and in no other way.

"He made Him who knew no sin to be sin for us." Jesus Christ went through identification with sin and put away sin on the Cross so that every person on earth might be freed from sin by the right of His Atonement. God made His own Son to be sin that He might make the sinner a saint—"that we might become the righteousness of God in Him" (2 Cor. 5:21).

The key to the missionary message is not human views or predilections regarding redemption but the revelation given by our Lord Himself concerning His life and death, "the Son of Man came . . . to give His life a ransom for many" (Matt. 20:28). When the Holy Spirit comes in He brings us the key to the missionary message, which is not the proclaiming of any particular view of salvation, but the proclaiming of "the Lamb of God who takes away the sin of the world." The Holy Spirit sheds abroad the love of God in our hearts, and the love of God is world-wide; there is no patriotism in the missionary message. This does not mean that patriots do not become missionaries but it does mean that the missionary message is not patriotic. The missionary message is irrespective of all race conditions; it is for the whole world. "God so loved the world."

Sin against Christ the Lamb of God is world-wide, the propitiation of Christ is worldwide, and the missionary's message is worldwide; it is a message not of condemnation, but of remission. "That repentance and remission of sins should be preached in His name to all nations" (Luke 24:47).

The only final thing in the world is redemption of Jesus Christ.

The limitless significance of the sermon on Christ—John 1:29.

The significance of the sermon on Christ the Lamb of God is limitless because He is the Lamb of God, not of humanity. "Behold! The Lamb of God who takes away the sin of the world!" The Bible reveals all through that our Lord bore the sin of the world by identification, not by sympathy. He came here for one purpose only—to bear away the sin of the world in His own person on the cross. He came to redeem, not to set a wonderful example. We have to beware of becoming the advocates of a certain view of the limitless. The redemption avails for everyone: "The Lamb of God who takes away the sin of the world," not the sin of those who belong to any particular country, but the sin of the world. The words are worthy only of Almighty God's wisdom, not of humanity's.

The Regenerative Magnitude of the Mission

". . . preached in His name among all the nations, beginning at Jerusalem."

"These are the ones who follow the Lamb wherever He goes" (Rev. 14:4). These words form a magnificent commentary on sacramental preaching, that is, preaching in His name.

The personal possession of the nature of the Lamb of God—Jesus spoke these words to His disciples and to no one else. To be a disciple means to be a believer in Jesus—one who has given up the right to self to the ownership of Christ. "You must possess My nature in yourselves," says Jesus, "then go and preach in My name—in My nature."

The powerful program of the naiveté of the Lamb of God—Naiveté means natural simplicity and unreservedness of thought, the divine simplicity of the phrase, "preached in His name." It is entirely free from diplomacy in any shape or form. The amazing simplicity of the nature of God is foolish judged by human wisdom; but "the foolishness of God is wiser than men" (1 Cor. 1:25).

The key to the missionary message is the proclamation of this gospel of propitiation for the sins of the whole world. We must be careful lest we become too wise for Jesus and say, "Oh but the people will never understand." We should say, "God knows how to make them understand therefore we will do what He tells us." If we have got hold of the truth of God for ourselves we have to give it out and not try to explain it. It is our explanations of God's truth that befog others. Let the truth come out in all its rugged force and strength and it will take effect in its own way. "That repentance and remission of sins should be preached. . . ." We are not to preach the doing of good things; good deeds are not to be preached, they are to be performed.

The particular place of the negotiations of the Lamb of God—"Among all the nations, beginning at Jerusalem." The particular place where our Lord tells His disciples to begin is where He is not believed in; and we do not need to go to the back of beyond for that. The first place may be inside our own skulls, in the intellect that will not believe in Him. If we remain true to Jesus Christ and to His command to preach in His name it will mean encountering hostility when we come in contact with the culture and wisdom and education that is not devoted to Jesus.

The Responsive Martyrdom of the Missionary
"And you are witnesses of these things" (Luke 24:48).

These imperative words are spoken to Jesus Christ's disciples. Witnesses are those who deliberately give up their lives to the ownership of another, not to a cause, and death will never make them swerve from their allegiance.

The wonder of witnessing—"Behold, I send the Promise of My Father upon you" (v. 49).

And in Acts 1:8 Jesus tells them what the result of the coming of the promise of the Father will be, "you shall be witnesses to Me." Many are prevented from being witnesses to Jesus by over-zealousness for His cause. "What are you being trained for? Are you going to be a minister, a deaconess, a missionary? What is the use of all this training?" Bible training and missionary training are not meant to train people for a purpose for which human nature can train itself. Religious institutions start out on the right line of making witnesses to Jesus, then they get swept off on to the human line and begin to train people for certain things, to train for a cause, or a special enterprise, or for a denomination, and the more these training places are multiplied the less chance is there of witnesses to Jesus being made. Today we are in danger of reversing Jesus Christ's order. There stands the eternal Word of Christ, "As the Father has sent Me, I also send you" (John 20:21). Too often a missionary is sent first by a denomination, and secondly by Christ. We may talk devoutly about Jesus in our meetings, but He has to take the last place.

One way in which Satan comes as an angel of light to Christians today is by telling them there is no need to use their minds. We must use our minds; we must keep the full power of our intellect ablaze for God on any subject that awakens us in our study of His Word, always keeping the secret of the life hid with Christ in God. Think of the sweat and labor and agony of nerve that a scientific student will go through in order to attain an end; then think of the slipshod, lazy way we go into work for God.

The woe of witnessing—A missionary is one who is wedded to the charter of his Lord and Master. "I determined not to know anything among you except Jesus Christ and Him crucified" (1 Cor. 2:2). It is easier to belong to a coterie and tell what God has done for us, or to become a devotee to divine healing, or to a special type of sanctification. Paul did not say woe is me if I do not preach what Jesus Christ has done for me, but, "Woe is me if I do not preach the gospel" (1 Cor. 9:16). Personal experience is a mere illustration that explains the wonderful difference the gospel has made in us. Our experience is the gateway into the gospel for us, but it is not the gospel. This is the gospel: "That repentance and remission of sins should be preached in His name."

The worship of witnessing—Worship is the love offering of our keen sense of the worth-ship of God. True worship springs from the same source as the missionary himself. To worship God truly is to become a missionary because our worship is a testimony to Him. It is presenting back to God the best He has given to us, publicly, not privately. Every act of worship is a public testimony and is at once the most personally sacred and the most public act that God demands of His faithful ones.

The Lock for the Missionary Key
Romans 10:14–15

The Discovered Sense of Responsibility
How then shall they call . . . ?

The awakened sense of responsibility to God for the whole world is seen in the rousing up of the Christian community in sympathy towards the missionary enterprise. In recent years missionary organization, from the human standpoint, has almost reached the limit of perfection. But if all this perfection of organization does is to make people discover a new sense of responsibility without an emphatic basing of everything on redemption, it will end in a gigantic failure. Today many are interested in the foreign field because of a passionate interest in something other than the Lord Jesus and His command, "Go therefore and make disciples." All this organization ought to mean that we can go ahead as never before; but if the dethronement of Jesus creeps in the finest organization will but perfect the lock which cannot open of itself.

There are wonderful things about light, but there are terrible things also. When once the light of God's Spirit breaks into a heart and life that has been perfectly happy and peaceful without God, it is hell for that one. "If I had not come and spoken to them, they would have no sin" (John 15:22). If we take this aspect of things out of the individual setting and put it into a universal setting, we shall see the reason of the antipathy to foreign missions. It is because light brings confusion and disaster. The light produces hell where before there was peace; it produces pain where before there was death. God's method in the pathway of light is destructive before it is constructive. The missionary is the incarnation of Holy Spirit light and when he or she comes all the things of the night tremble. The night of unbelief is being split up not by the incoming of civilization, but by the witness of men and women who are true to God.

In this country we know nothing about what Jesus mentions in Matt. 10:34–39, but wherever the missionary brings the evangel of Jesus, it will have to be faced. Those who become converts to Jesus have to go through these things literally; they are persecuted and flung out. Unless missionaries know God and trust in Him entirely, they will step down to a lower level and compromise and tell the people they need not do certain things in exactly the way that Jesus indicates. But if they stand true to God they will preach the truth at whatever cost to the converts. No nervous system can stand that strain, no sensitivity of mind can stand that test. No one but the Holy Spirit can stand it, because He has the mind of God.

The Discovered Service of Reasonableness
How shall they believe . . .?

Never before has there been such an educated and reasonable and intense grasp of all the problems, social and international and personal, as there is today. Everything has been laid at the service of the missionary. The opportunity is one that makes us hold our breath with amazement, and at the same moment sink back. But who has the key? All the forces of civilization and education and healing are in perfect trim; the fullness of time has come as never before; the only thing that is lacking is the key that fits the lock. Today the emphasis is on the reasonable aspects of missionary work, the healing, civilizing, and educating. These are all admirable and if the keys were used they would facilitate rapidly our Lord's purpose and make it much easier to get into the heart of the problem; but the danger is that we have forgotten the key. The key is the Lordship of Jesus Christ and His supreme authority.

The Discovered Scheme of Representatives
How shall they hear . . .?

There is nothing more thrilling than the realization of what is at the disposal of the Christian church today. Every element of science, skill, and learning has been taxed to its limit to serve the missionary in order that the world might hear, but, "How shall they hear without a preacher?" The work that is being done cannot be too highly praised, but it is not preaching. "Woe is me if I do not preach the gospel," that was the burning message of the apostle Paul. In spite of all the perfection of organization, the magnificent equipment, and tremendous resolve, the purpose for which the whole thing was started is frequently not fulfilled and the scheme ends simply as something to be admired. That accounts for the alternation of exaltation and despair. Just when everything seems ripe for God and our hopes are raised to the highest pitch we are suddenly chilled because there is no message, nothing to be believed, nothing for the world to hear. Our organization has enabled us to rearrange and systematize the problems but it cannot solve the problems. It is not that the scheme is wrong. What is wrong is that the key has been lost, the lordship of Jesus Christ has been forgotten; His supreme authority over the missionary has been ignored, He is not realized as King of kings.

Out of the center of His own agony in the Garden our Lord counsels us to "watch and pray, lest you enter into temptation" (Matt. 26:41). Missionary enterprise will reveal more quickly than anything whether we have been caught by the lure of wrong roads to the kingdom. When we pray "Your kingdom come," we have to see that we allow the King to have His way in us first, that we ourselves are personally related to Him by sanctification. God's plan is that the truth must die—"Unless a grain of wheat falls into the ground and dies, it remains alone . . ." (John 12:24). Christian work, if it is spiritual, has followed that law at home and everywhere because that is the only way in which it can bring forth God's fruit.

The Discovered Source of Reserves
How shall they preach . . . ?

A missionary is one sent by Jesus Christ as the Father sent Him. Our Lord's first obedience was not to the needs of human beings but to the will of His Father, and the first great duty of the Christian is not to the needs of mankind, but to the will of the Lord. To elevate the unbelieving, to lift up the downtrodden and oppressed, is magnificent but it is not the reason for missionary enterprise. The teaching of the New Testament is that we ought to be doing all these things to the best of our ability, but missionary enterprise is another thing. A missionary is one who is fitted with the key to the missionary lock while pursuing the ordinary callings of life.

What is needed today is Christian sociology, not sociology Christianized. One way in which God will reintroduce the emphasis on the gospel is by bringing into His service men and women who not only understand the problems, but who have learned that the secret of the whole thing is supernatural regeneration, that is, personal holiness wrought by the grace of God.

Jesus Christ came to do what no human being can do, He came to redeem people, to alter their dispositions, to plant in them the Holy Spirit, to make them new creatures. Christianity is not the obliteration of the old, but the transfiguration of the old.

Jesus Christ did not come to teach us to be holy; He came to make us holy. His teaching has no meaning for us unless we enter into His life by means of His death.

The Cross is the great central point. Jesus Christ is not first a teacher, He is first a Savior; and the thing that tells in the long run in a missionary's life is not successful understanding of His teaching, but the realization in one's personal life of the meaning of the Cross. There is only One who saves, and that is God. Missionaries are there to proclaim the marvel of that salvation, and what they proclaim becomes a sacrament within them. They are made the incarnation of what they preach. Missionaries will be put into places where they have to stand alone because they are being held true to the content of the gospel as it is in Jesus. There is a loneliness which comes from a defiant heroism which has no element of the gospel in it.

There is no more wholesome training for the foreign field than doing our duty in the home field. The foreign field is apt to have a glamour over it because it is away somewhere else. There is an inspiration and a sense of the heroic about going to the foreign field—until we get there, and find that the most terrible things we ever touched at home were clean and vigorous compared to the corruption that has to be faced there. Unless the life of a missionary is hid with Christ in God before work begins, that life will become exclusive and narrow; it will never become the servant of all, it will never wash the feet of others. Therefore we come back to the first principles. "The nations shall know that I am the Lord . . . when I am hallowed in you before their eyes" (Ezek. 36:23).

The Discovered Supremacy of Redemption

"How beautiful are the feet of those who preach the gospel of peace, who bring glad tidings of good things!" (Rom. 10:15).

Thank God for the countless numbers of individuals who realize that the only reality is redemption; that the only thing to preach is the gospel; that the only service to be rendered is the sacramental service of identification with our Lord's death and resurrection. To preach the gospel is to proclaim that God saves from sin and regenerates into His kingdom anyone and everyone who believes on the Lord Jesus. It means even more—it means to "disciple all the nations," not only on the authority of Jesus, but on the flesh and blood evidence of entire sanctification in the life of the missionary. "When it pleased God . . . to reveal His Son in me, that I might preach Him among the Gentiles" (Gal. 1:15–16).

Thus we end where we began, with our Lord Jesus Christ. He is the First and the Last; and laying His hands on the missionary He says, "Fear not, I have the keys."

The Key to Missionary Devotion

3 John 7

We live in a complex world amid such a mass of sensibilities and impressions that we are apt to imagine that it is the same with God. It is our complicated rationalism that makes the difficulty. We have to beware of every simplicity saving the simplicity that is in Christ.

The key to missionary devotion is put in our hands at the outset, "They went forth for His name's sake." The key is amazingly simple, as is everything connected with our Lord. Our difficulties arise when we lose the key, and we lose the key by not being simple.

The Domination of the Master Himself

John 21:15-16

The Master dominates, not domineers over, His disciples. His is the domination of holy love. If , for one moment, we see the Lord we may fall and slip away but we shall never rest until we find Him again. The destiny of every human being depends on a relationship to Jesus Christ; it is not on a relationship to life, or on service or usefulness, but simply and solely on a relationship to Jesus Christ.

Love for Him—"Simon, son of Jonah, do you love Me more than these?" (v. 15).

The sovereign preference of the disciple's person must be for the person of the Lord Jesus over every other preference. This preference for Him is first and last against all competition. Love is difficult to define, although simple to know; life is difficult to define, although simple to have. What we obtain we can to a certain extent define; but all we have as a personal inheritance is indefinable. Intellect and logic are instruments, they are not life. The tyranny of the intellectual Napoleon is that one makes out that the intellect is life. Intellect is the expression of life. In the same way, theology is said to be religion; theology is the instrument of religion.

Love cannot be defined. Try and define your love for Jesus Christ and you will find you cannot do it. Love is the sovereign preference of my person for another person, and Jesus Christ demands that other person be Himself. That does not mean we have no preference for anyone else but that Jesus Christ has the sovereign preference; within that sovereign preference come all other loving preferences, down to flowers and animals. The Bible makes no distinction between divine love and human love, it speaks only of love.

When a disciple is dominated by love to Jesus Christ, he or she is not always conscious of Him. It is absurd to think that we have to be conscious all the time of the one we love most. The one we are conscious of is the one we do not love most. The child is not conscious all the time of love for the mother; it is the crisis that produces the consciousness. When we are getting into the throes of love, we are conscious of it because we are not in love yet. We imagine that we have to take God into our consciousness, whereas God takes us into His consciousness; consequently we are rarely conscious of Him.

Love to Him—" 'Simon, son of Jonah, do you love me?' He said to Him, 'Yes, Lord; You know that I love You.' "

In v. 15 our Lord had made a comparison—"Do you love Me more than these?" To demand a declaration of love beyond comparison is to risk losing all.

Missionaries must be dominated by this love beyond compare to the Lord Jesus Christ otherwise they will be simply the servants of a denomination or a cause, or seekers for relief from crushing sorrow in work. Many go into Christian work not for the sake of His name, but in order to find surcease from their own sorrow because of unrequited love, or because of a bereavement, or a disappointment. Such workers are not dominated by the Master and they are likely to strew the mission field with failure and sighs, and to discourage those who work with them. There is only one thing stronger than any of these things, and that is love.

Love in Him—"He said to him the third time, 'Simon, son of Jonah, do you love Me?' "

Our Lord's question elicited the amazed confession of Peter's deepest heart—"Lord, You know all things; You know that I love You." Peter did not say, "Look at this and that," to confirm it. Love never professes; love confesses. "Peter was grieved because He said to him the third time." Our Lord's thrice repeated question revealed to Peter's own soul that there was no one he loved more than Jesus, and in utter amazement as he looked at himself in his grief, he said, "You know that I love You." When the domination of the Master over the heart of a disciple reaches the depth of that expression then He entrusts His call to that one: "Feed my sheep."

"Do you love me? . . . Feed my sheep." Our Lord indicated three times how love to Himself is to be manifested in the life of the lover—in identification with His interests in others. Our Lord does not ask us to die for Him but to identify ourselves with His interests in other people—not identify Him with our interests in other people. "Feed my sheep." "See that they get nourished in their knowledge of Me."

Paul, in 1 Corinthians 13:4–8, gives the charter of love. "Love suffers long and is kind . . . thinks no evil. . . . Love never fails." The love of God is wrought in us by the Holy Spirit. He sheds abroad the love of God, the nature of God in our hearts, and that love works efficaciously through us as we come in contact with others. The test of love for Jesus Christ is the practical one, all the rest is sentimental jargon.

The Domination of the Master's Name
Matt. 28:18-20

"Make disciples of all the nations." That cannot be done unless Jesus Christ is who He says He is. The apostolic office is not based on faith, but on love. The two working lines for carrying out Jesus Christ's command are, first, the sovereign preference of our person for the person of Jesus Christ; and second, the willing and deliberate identification of our interests with Jesus Christ's interests in other people. Ardor must never be mistaken for love, nor the sense of the heroic for devotion to Jesus, nor self-sacrifice for fulfilling a spiritual destiny. It is much easier to follow in the track of the heroic than to remain true to Jesus in drab, mean streets. Human nature unaided by God can do the heroic business; human pride unaided by God can do the self-sacrificing (see 1 Cor. 8:1-3); but it takes the supernatural power of God to keep us as saints in the drab commonplace days. The need can never be the call for missionary enterprise. The need is the opportunity. The call is the commission of Jesus Christ and relationship to His person. "All authority has been given to Me. . . . Go therefore." Any work for God that has less than a passion for Jesus Christ as its motive will end in crushing heartbreak and discouragement.

Loyalty to His character—"All authority has been given to Me."
Loyalty to the Master's character means that the missionary believes in the Lord's almightiness on earth as well as in heaven,

though every common sense, rational fact should declare loudly that He has no more power than a morning mist. If we are going to be loyal to Jesus Christ's character as it is portrayed in the New Testament, we have a tremendously big task on hand. Loyalty to Jesus is the thing that halts us today. People will be loyal to work, to ideals, to anything, but they are not willing to acknowledge loyalty to Jesus Christ.

Christian workers frequently become intensely impatient of this idea of loyalty to Jesus. Our Lord is dethroned more emphatically by Christian workers than by the world. Loyalty to Jesus is the outcome of the indwelling of the personal Holy Spirit working in us the supernatural redemption of Christ, and keeping us true to His name when every common sense fact gives the lie to it. In Ps. 63, the psalmist says that he nearly lost his faith in God because every rational fact seemed to prove that he had trusted a fiction. There is no test to equal the test of remaining loyal to Jesus Christ's character when the ungodly are in the ascendant. We are apt to become cynical, and a cynical view is always a distorted view, a view arising out of pique because some personal object is being thwarted.

Loyalty to His call—"Go therefore, and make disciples of all the nations . . ."

Loyalty to the call of our Lord means not merely that we keep the letter of His command, but that we keep in contact with His nature, that is, His name. "Unless you . . . become as little children" (Matt. 18:3). The meaning of new birth is receiving His nature. The call of the sea, the call of the mountains, the call of the wild—all of these calls are perfectly in accord with the nature of the one who listens. Everyone does not hear the call of the sea, only the one who has the nature of the sea within. The call of the mountains does not come to everyone, only to the one who has the nature of the mountains within.

Likewise, the call of God does not come to everyone. It comes only to those who have the nature of God in them. The call of Jesus Christ does not come to everyone, only to those who have His nature. Our loyalty is not to stand by the letter of what Jesus says but to keep our souls continually open to the nature of the Lord Jesus Christ.

Loyalty to His commission—". . . teaching them to observe all things that I have commanded you."

Loyalty to the commission means, first of all, that missionaries set themselves to find out all that the Lord taught. There is not a greater test for loyal concentration than that. Jesus did not say teach salvation, or teach sanctification, or teach divine healing, but teach "them to observe all things that I have commanded you" (Matt. 28:20). There is no room for the specialist or the crank or the fanatic in missionary work. A fanatic is one who has forgotten to be a human being. Our Lord never sent out cranks and fanatics, He sent out those who were loyal to His domination. He sent out ordinary men and women, plus dominating devotion to Himself by the indwelling Holy Spirit.

Missionaries are not sent by Jesus Christ to do medical work, educational work, industrial work; all that is part of the ordinary duty of life, and they ought to be so equipped that they do these things naturally. But Jesus Christ never sends His disciples to do these things; He sends His disciples to teach, to "make disciples of all the nations."

The Detachment for the Master
John 21:18–22

This detachment to Jesus is rarely referred to; it means personal attachment to no one and to nothing saving our Lord

Himself. Our Lord did not teach detachment from other things; He taught attachment to Himself. Jesus Christ was not a recluse. He did not cut Himself off from society, He was amazingly in and out among the ordinary things of life; but He was disconnected fundamentally from it all. He was not aloof but He lived in another world. His life was so social that critics called Him a glutton and a winebibber, a friend of publicans and sinners. His detachments were inside, toward God.

Our external detachments are often an indication of secret, vital attachment to the things from which we keep away externally. Before we are rightly detached to Jesus Christ, we spend our time keeping ourselves detached from other things, which is a sure sign of a secret affinity with them. When we are really detached to Jesus He can entrust us with all other things. "See, we have left all, and followed You" (Matt. 19:27), said Peter, implying, "What will we get?" Jesus told him that they would get a hundred times more of all they had given up, once the detachment to Himself had been formed.

The life sacrificed—"Most assuredly, I say to you, when you were younger, you girded yourself, and walked where you wished; but when you are old, you will stretch out your hands, and another will gird you and carry you where you do not wish" (John 21:18).

These words are a description of the nature of internal sacrifice and every unspiritual desire will plead against the undesirability of the sacrifice. "God could never expect me to give up my magnificent respect and devote my life to the missionary cause." But He happens to have done so. The battle is yours. He says no more, but He waits.

The life sacramented—"This He spoke, signifying by what death he would glorify God. And when He had spoken this, He said to him, 'Follow Me.' "

Three irrational conclusions—death, glorifying God, following Jesus, and at His ascension Jesus disappeared. Our Lord never talked on the basis of reason, He talked on the basis of redemption. What is nonsense rationally is redemptive reality. The "Follow Me," spoken three years before had nothing mystical in it, it was an external following; now it is a following in internal martyrdom.

Sacramented means that the elements of the natural life are presenced by divinity as they are broken in God's service providentially. We have to be entirely adjusted into Jesus before He can make us a sacrament. The missionary must be a sacramental personality, one through whom the presence of God comes to others.

The life sacred—"Jesus said to him, 'If I will that he remain till I come, what is that to you? You follow Me.' "

Not only is the life of the missionary sacred to God, but the lives of others are sacred also, and when one tries to pry into another's concerns one will receive the rebuke of our Lord, "What is that to you? You follow Me."

His!

"They were Yours, You gave them to Me" (John 17:6).

It is this aspect of a disciple's life that is frequently forgotten. We are apt to think of ourselves as our own, of the work as our work. A great point in spiritual nobility has been reached when we can really say, "I am not my own." It is only the noble nature that can be mastered—an unpalatable truth if we are spiritually stiffnecked and stubborn, refusing to be mastered. The Son of God is the Highest of all, yet the characteristic of His life was obedience. We have to learn that God is not meant for us, it is we who are meant for God. Jesus Christ does satisfy the last, aching abyss of the human heart, but that must never lead to thinking of God the Father, God the Son, and God the Holy Spirit as an almighty arrangement for satisfying us. "Do you not know that . . . you are not your own?" (1 Cor. 6:19). It is this realization that is wrought in us by the Holy Spirit.

His! Does that apply to us? Have we realized that our bodies are not our own, but His, temples of the Holy Spirit. Have we realized that our hearts and affections are not our own, but His? If so, we shall be careful over inordinate affection. Have we realized that all the ambitions of life are His? We are out for one thing only, for Jesus Christ's enterprises. This is the inner secret of the missionary—I know that I am His and that He is carrying on His enterprises through me; I am His possession and He can do as He likes with me.

Each one has a setting of difficulties and temptations, and so it is with the missionary. If we cannot live at home as His, we shall find it much more difficult to live in the foreign field as His; we shall be more likely to make things ours than to remain loyal to Him. If we have been "wobblers" at home, we shall be wobblers out there. If we have learned to face ourselves with God at home, we shall face ourselves with God out there. But we have to learn to do it, and it is not easy at the beginning. Where they are placed is a matter of indifference to missionaries; if they maintain contact with God out of them will flow rivers of living water. We have the idea that we engineer missionary enterprise; but it is the genius of the Holy Spirit that makes us go. God does not do anything with us, only through us; consequently the one thing God estimates in His servants is the work of the Holy Spirit.

Jesus Christ is the only One who has the right to tell us what it means to be His, and in Luke 14:26–33 He set down the conditions of discipleship. These conditions are summed up in one astounding word—hate. "If anyone comes to Me and does not hate (that is, hate every good thing that divides the heart from loyalty to Jesus) . . . he cannot be My disciple" (v. 26). Every one of the relationships Jesus mentions may be a competitive relationship. We may prefer to be our mother's, or our father's, or our own, and Jesus does not say we cannot be but He does say he cannot be My disciple; he cannot be one over whom Jesus writes the word hate.

In verses 28–33 our Lord was not referring to a cost the disciple has to estimate but stating that He has estimated the cost. Jesus Christ is not less than a human being among humans, and He has counted the cost; that is why He made the conditions so stern. Those who say, "Lord, Lord," are not the ones Jesus takes on His enterprises; He takes only those in whom He has done everything; they are the ones on whom He can rely. Many devote themselves to work for God in whom Jesus Christ has done nothing; consequently they bungle His business, run up the white flag to the prince of this world and compromise with him. Jesus said that the only ones He will take on His building and battling enterprises are those who are devoted to Him because He has altered their dispositions.

The Missionary Watching

"Watch with Me" (Matt. 26:40).

Watch with no private point of view of your own; watch entirely with Me. In the early stages of Christian experience we do not watch with Jesus, we watch for Him. We do not know how to watch with Jesus in the circumstances of our lives, in the revelation of His Word; we have the idea only of His watching with us, answering our problems, helping us. But Jesus says, "Watch with Me." How is it possible to watch with One whom we do not understand? The early disciples did not understand Jesus in the slightest. They had been with Him for three years, they loved Him to the limit of their natural hearts, but they had no idea what He meant when He talked of His kingdom or of His Cross. Jesus was inscrutable to them on these main points. They could not watch with Him for the simple reason that they did not know what He was after. They could not watch with Him in His Gethsemane, they did not know why He was suffering, and they slept for their own sorrow. Then Jesus gave Himself up and they all forsook Him and fled, and when they saw Him put to death on the cross their hearts were broken. Then after the Resurrection, Jesus came to them and said, "Receive the Holy Spirit" (John 20:22), and they learned to watch with Him all the rest of their lives.

The real center of the disciple's devotion is watching with Jesus. When we have learned to watch with Him the thought of self is not kept down because it is not there to keep down; self-effacement is complete. Self has been effaced by the deliberate giving up to another self in sovereign preference, and the manifestation of the life in the actual whirl of things is, "I am not my own, but His."

The Missionary Waiting

"Because you have kept My command to persevere" (Rev. 3:10).

This is not the patience of pessimism, nor of exhaustion, but the patience of joyfulness because God reigns. It may be illustrated by likening the saint to a bow and arrow in the hands of God. God is aiming at His mark, and He stretches and strains until the saint says, "I cannot stand any more," but God does not heed. He goes on stretching until His purpose is in sight, then He lets fly, and the arrow reaches His mark.

Moses "endured as seeing Him who is invisible" (Heb. 11:27). The vision of God is the source of the patience of a saint. A person with the vision of God is not devoted simply to a cause or to a particular issue, but to God Himself. Our Lord sent none out on the ground of what He had done for them, but only because they had seen Him, and by the power of His Spirit had perceived who He is. Nothing can daunt the one who has seen Jesus. Someone who has only a personal testimony as to what Jesus can do may be daunted; but nothing can turn the individual who has seen Him. It takes the endurance which comes from a vision of God to go on without seeing results. We are not here for successful service, but to be faithful.

Had Jesus any results? Before we go into work for Him we must learn that the disciple is not above his Master. We cannot be discouraged if we belong to Him, for it was said of Him, "He will not fail nor be discouraged" (Isa. 42:4). Discouragement is "disenchanted egotism." Things are not happening the way I expected they would, therefore I am going to give it all up. To talk like that is a sure sign that we are not possessed by love for Him, but only by love for ourselves. Discouragement always comes when we insist on having our own way.

The Missionary Worshiping

"Worship God in the Spirit" (Phil. 3:3).

Circumcision is the Old Testament symbol for New Testament sanctification. To worship God in the Spirit is not to worship Him sincerely, in the remote part of our nature, but to worship Him by the power of the Spirit He gives to us. The Holy Spirit never becomes our spirit; He quickens our spirit into oneness with God. Worship is the tryst of sacramental identification with God; we deliberately give back to God the best He has given us that we may be identified with Him in it. "I beseech you . . . present your bodies a living sacrifice . . . which is your spiritual worship" (Rom. 12:1, RV). Worship of God is the sacramental element in a saint's life. We have to give back to God in worship every blessing He has given to us.

The Missionary Witnessing

"But you shall receive power when the Holy Spirit has come upon you; and you shall be witnesses to Me" (Acts 1:8).

The Holy Spirit is the One who expounds the nature of Jesus to us. When the Holy Spirit comes in, He does infinitely more than deliver us from sin; He makes us one with our Lord. "Witnesses to Me," a satisfaction to Jesus wherever He places us. To be a witness means to live a life of unsullied, uncompromising, and unbribed devotion to Jesus. A true witness is one who lets the light shine in works that exhibit the disposition of Jesus. Our Lord makes the one who is a witness His own possession, He becomes responsible for that one.

We have to be entirely His, to exhibit His Spirit no matter what circumstances we are in. It is extraordinary to watch God alter things. We have to worship God in the difficult circumstances, and when He chooses He will alter them in two seconds. If we deliberately sign ourselves as "His," then all that happens is the fulfillment of our Lord's own words in Matthew 11:28–30: "Come to Me . . . and I will give you rest. Take My yoke upon you, and learn from Me . . . and you will find rest for your souls."

> Christ! I am Christ's! and let the name suffice you,
>> Ay, for me too He greatly hath sufficed;
> Lo with no winning words, I would entice you,
>> Paul has no honour and no friend but Christ.

> Yea, thro' life, death, thro' sorrow and thro' sinning
>> He shall suffice me, for He hath sufficed:
> Christ is the end, for Christ was the beginning,
> Christ the beginning, for the end is Christ.

WORKMEN OF GOD

How to Work for the Cure of Souls

"And David said, 'There is none like it; give it to me' "
—1 Samuel 21:9.

The setting is known to us all. David was talking about Goliath's sword, and he asked for it, "give it to me." We read the passage in Deuteronomy where Moses said to the children of Israel, "the case that is too hard for you, bring to me, and I will hear it" (1:17). I want to take these two Old Testament mighty men of God as types of what the worker for God must be like to work for the cure of souls.

With regard to the sword, that there is none like it, if you will turn to Heb. 4:12, you will see how I want to take Goliath's sword and spiritualize it in the hands of a worker for God among humankind: "For the word of God is living and powerful, and sharper than any two-edged sword, piercing even to the division of soul and spirit, and of joints and marrow, and is a discerner of the thoughts and intents of the heart." It is quite obvious that if you are not David and are trying to use Goliath's sword, you will do far more harm to yourself than damage to the enemy. You must be the direct line of succession to David. David and Moses were mighty giants, but we have to be of the same family connection. What is the same family connection in this dispensation? Why, those who are born again of the Spirit of God, and those who are so identified with the Lord Jesus that they have entered into the experience of entire sanctification. When they use the Word of God they do not damage themselves, nor hurt other souls; but they do great damage to the kingdom of the devil and bring benefit to the souls of human beings.

Before we take up the question of the kind of souls we shall have to deal with, we must deal with the worker. There are big difficulties in the way. The first difficulty is that we are not dealing with people's bodies. If we were, we could be taught in special schools and colleges, trained and developed in such a way that we would know fairly well how to apply principles to the various ailments of people, because physical ailments have a wonderful likeness to each other. This has led many Christian workers astray; they think that because people's bodies and bodily ailments are alike, and because one cure, carefully and judiciously prescribed by a physician who diagnosed the case aright was successful and can be applied to other cases with similar results, that people's souls can be treated in the same way. But you cannot deal with the human soul and with the ailments and difficulties of the human soul according to any principle whatever. I think that any of you who have worked for God know this, that when you get into the way of using certain verses of Scripture and applying them to those who are seeking new birth, and certain other verses to those seeking sanctification, you will find suddenly that God's Spirit will depart from you and He will not use those verses in your hands anymore. The reason is this: that as soon as we get wedded to a shortcut in dealing with souls, God leaves us alone.

The first thing I want to lay down for workers (I am talking about ones who really are born again of the Spirit of God and have been entirely sanctified) is that he or she must rely on the Holy Spirit to direct as to what to say in the case of every soul that comes. Do not rely on your memory, do not remember how you dealt with cases in the past, but recognize and rely on the Holy Spirit—that He will bring to your remembrance the particular verse for you to apply at this time. You will find over and over again that God will bring confusion to your methods and will make you apply a text to sanctification which you in your system have said can only be applied to new birth; and He will make you apply a text which you have said can only apply to sanctification to something else, and you will make incessant blunders in work for God if you are not careful and watchful and heedful of the guidance of the Holy Spirit and of His bringing the Word of God to your remembrance. Remember, then, that the worker who is rightly related to God must ever rely on the Holy Spirit for guidance in each individual case.

Then, I want to apply Moses' statement: "The case that is too hard for you, bring to me." Do you know how to bring your cases to God? We all know how to bring them to one another and how to talk to Christian workers about dealing with souls, but just as there are quack doctors in the medical profession, so there is the same thing in the spiritual domain. Beware of anything that does not fling you straight back in reliance on the Holy Spirit as the most practical factor you know in bringing to your remembrance the Word of God and how to apply it.

Then another thing:the worker must live among the facts he or she has to deal with. Regarding the training of workers, take the highest class we know of: ministers. One of the greatest difficulties in most of our colleges for training ministers who are supposed to work for the cure of souls is that they are never taught how to deal with souls. There is hardly a college anywhere for training ministers where the question of dealing with souls is ever mentioned. Ministers will bear me out in this, that everything they have learned they have had to learn out of their own experience. They are trained in everything but how to deal with the facts they have to deal with.

There are two kinds of facts the worker must be among—one must go to school among human souls. I mean we must keep ourselves in touch, not with theories, but with people, and never get out of touch with human beings if we are going to use the Word of God skillfully among them, and if the Holy Spirit is to apply the Word of God through us as workers who do not need to be ashamed (see 2 Tim. 2:15). Live among your human facts and you will find how continually God stirs up your nest. If you are a worker He will constantly surround you with different kinds of people with different difficulties, and He will constantly put you to school among those facts. He will keep you in contact with human stuff, and human stuff is very sordid; in fact, human stuff is made of just the same stuff as you and I are made of; do not shut yourself away from it. Beware of the tendency to live a life apart and shut away. Get among people. Jesus prayed, "I do not pray that You should take them out of the world, but that You should keep them from the evil one" (John 17:15).

Then there is another series of facts: Bible facts. We have to go to school among human souls, and we have to educate ourselves in Bible facts. A remarkable thing about this Book of God (and I hope, by God's grace, to point this out) is that for every type of individual we come across there is a distinct, clear line laid down here as to the way to apply God's truth to it. The stupid soul, the stubborn soul, the soul that is mentally diseased, the soul that is convicted of sin, the soul with the twisted mind, the sensual soul—every one of the facts that you meet in your daily walk and business has its counterpart here, and God has a word and a revelation fact with regard to every life you come across. Let me emphasize these three things again: First, the Christian worker who is right with God must rely every moment on the Holy Spirit when dealing with another soul. Second, the worker must live among human facts, men and women, not theories. Do not let us tell ourselves what men and women are like, let us find out what they are like. One of the greatest mistakes in the world is to tell yourself what a person is like; you do not know what that one is like. The only One who can teach you how to deal with the various specimens around you is the Holy Spirit. The third thing is ransack this old Book from cover to cover in the most practical way you know—by using a concordance, by rewriting the Psalms, or by any other immediate, practical method.

I know it is customary to ridicule certain ways in which some people say God guides them, but I am very chary about ridiculing any methods. For example, it is easy to ridicule this kind of method: "Lord, direct me to a word, I am just going to shut my eyes and open the Book and put my finger on a passage." I say it is easy to ridicule it, yet it is absurd to say that God has not led people in that way; He has. Why I mention these facts is to knock certain theories to pieces. You cannot tie God down to a particular line. You will find that God does use the most extraordinary methods people adopt; only do not take anyone else's way, get to know how God deals with you, and how He deals with others through you in the most practical way.

Keep these three things in mind—reliance on the Holy Spirit of God, keeping in contact with people, and above all, keeping in contact with the revelation facts in God's Book; live among them, and ask God how to apply them.

Another thing I want to mention—never believe what people tell you about themselves. There is only one person in a thousand who can actually tell you his or her symptoms; and beware of the people who can tell you where they are spiritually. I mean by that, never be guided by what people tell you; rely on the Spirit of God all the time you are probing them.

Let me read you this in regard to medical treatment:

Recent evidence in the law courts has pointed to a fact which the medical profession holds of great value—the necessity, not only of personal and private interview with a patient, but of the penetrative ability to get at the real facts and symptoms. In other words, successful diagnosis depends on the doctor's acumen in cross-examination.

Cross-examination of a patient is almost always necessary," says an eminent medical man. "They will give me causes, or rather what they think are causes, instead of symptoms. The rich patient is more troublesome in this respect than the poor, for he has had leisure in which to evolve a sort of scheme of his illness, based on 'popular' medical knowledge.

Patients always color facts, speaking absolutely instead of relatively. They never tell the truth about the amount of sleep they have had or as to appetite. They frequently say they have had nothing to eat. Casually you find there were two eggs at least for breakfast. A minute or two later they remember stewed steak for dinner.

Perhaps the greatest need for cross-examination is that it gives an extended opportunity to the medical man to examine the patient objectively. The most important symptoms are generally those the patient never notices.

If that is true in the medical profession, which deals with people's bodies, it is a thousand times more true about spiritual symptoms when it comes to dealing with a person's soul. Do beware, then, of paying too much attention to the talk of the one who is in trouble, keep your own heart and mind alert on what God is saying to you; get to the place where you will know when the Holy Spirit brings the Word of God to your remembrance for that one.

There is a wrong use of God's Word, and a right one. The wrong use is this sort of thing: someone comes to you, and you cast about in your mind what sort of person he or she is, then hurl a text like a projectile, either in prayer or in talking as you deal with that one. That is a use of the Word of God that kills your own soul and the souls of the people you deal with. The Spirit of God is not in that. Jesus said, "The words that I speak to you are spirit, and they are life" (John 6:63). Paul said God "also made us sufficient as ministers of the new covenant, not of the letter but of the Spirit; for the letter kills, but the Spirit gives life" (2 Cor. 3:6). Do remember to keep your soul in unsullied touch with the directions of the Spirit.

Another thing that is very puzzling is this. Probably all of you have had experiences as I have on this line: you listen to clear Bible teaching, unmistakably clear, almost taking people by the hand and leading them straight into the kingdom of God, but they never come. Another time a speaker gets up and twists everything, and to your astonishment people are born again. That frequently happened in Water Street Mission in New York—some who had been wonderfully saved would get up and tell what they had been and what they are now, then others would do the same, and the Spirit of God got hold of the people. Before you knew where you were, out they came to the altar, and these rough people knelt down and prayed with them and they "struck something," as they say out there, and something "struck them," and they were wonderfully born again.

Now these are facts we have to look at. You cannot put God down to a prescribed method. These souls were real, living, good specimens of what God had done, and the Spirit of God worked through them. I mention that because it confuses a great amount of our reasoning in Christian work; over and over again you will find that some poor, ignorant servant or artisan, who seems scarcely to know how to put anything together, is used of God mightily in the salvation of souls; others have a clear understanding of the whole thing and put the way of salvation ever so clearly, yet nothing happens. So all we can get at is the main methods laid down in God's Book about the worker. Let us ask ourselves, "Do I experientially know what the salvation of

God is? Do I know what entire sanctification means in my own experience?" The worker for God must be in a healthy, vigorous spiritual condition.

I want to say one word of criticism about the choosing of Sunday school teachers. The way Sunday school teachers are chosen is that as soon as a person gets introduced into the kingdom of God, he or she is given a Sunday school class to teach. When you come to God's way, you will find something very different; when a soul gets introduced into the kingdom of God, that person has got to do something, but it is something along the line of the new life he or she has received—obedience and walking in the light—until the person is consolidated in the ways of God. Why is this necessary? Because dealing with souls is ten times more dangerous than dealing with bodies. Unless you are in a healthy, vigorous condition with God, you will catch the disease of the soul you are dealing with instead of helping to cure it. Unless you are out among the tremendous facts of God's revelation in the Bible, unless you know how to take breezy walks through that Book, unless you know how to walk up and down that country and take in the air of God's hills and get thoroughly robust, and continually change your walk among those facts, you are sure to catch the diseases of the souls you are dealing with. So remember, it is absolutely necessary to be like the cedars of Lebanon. Do you know the characteristic of a Lebanon tree? The cedars of Lebanon have such extraordinary power of life that instead of nourishing parasites they kill them, the life within is so strong and so robust that instead of feeding the parasites they choke them off. God grant that we may be so filled with His life, may flourish as the cedars of Lebanon, so that He can trust us down in all the dark, difficult places among the souls of our fellow human beings and be able to pour His tremendous health and power through us.

How sad it is to see men and women who did begin to work for God, and whose work God honored, slowly fall off. Why? They have caught the disease of death among the people they have been dealing with. In the medical profession, particularly doctors who deal with the insane have continually to be changed, continually shifted. Why? Because they take the diseases and troubles they live among, and you will find that God the Holy Spirit has an amazing power of shifting His workers. Some wonder why God keeps shifting them, why He shifts their circumstances; the reason is not only to keep them in touch with the great sphere of work, but to keep their souls alive.

Do remember, then, that it is necessary for the worker to be healthy, and beware of this mistake: that by working for God among people, you develop your own Christian life; you do not unless your Christian life is there first. It is so obvious that it needs to be said over again—you cannot develop your own Christian life unless it is there. The advice given that if you work for God you develop your own life often means that if you work for God you get right yourself; you do not, you have to be right with God first.

The next time you deal with a soul at the penitent form, remember it is one thing to tell a person to receive the Spirit of God, to recognize and rely on Him, but quite another thing for you to do the same thing. Unless you recognize the Spirit of God, and rely on Him, and expect Him to bring to your remembrance some word that is going to apply in that case, you will be of very little use as an expert soul-curer and for putting people in the way to get right with God.

Then do live among human facts! Thank God He has given the majority of us the surroundings of real, definite, sordid human beings; there is no pretense about them. The people we live among and come in contact with are not theories, they are facts. That is the kind of thing God wants us to keep among.

Then third, see that you get into this Book. I feel more than hungry to see men and women roused up to get hold of this Book and live among its facts; then the Spirit of God will bring to their remembrance how to apply the truth in each case.

The Worker Among
the Abnormal

"For the Son of Man has come to seek and to save that which was lost" (Luke 19:10).

Abnormal means not normal or according to rule, not upright, not good. God's Book says that the whole of the human race is abnormal.

In the first chapter we dealt with the Christian worker, and we found that, first of all one must have a definite experience in one's own life of the marvelous salvation of God; then, that one must learn how to recognize and rely on the Spirit of God in dealing with souls; one must live in the facts of the Bible, and keep in touch with the facts of human life. Now we deal with some of the facts of human life as God's Book reveals them.

I want to notice a very important distinction, that the lost, from the Bible standpoint, are not doomed. The lost Jesus Christ is seeking; the doomed are those who rebel against the seeking Savior. To Jesus Christ all are lost, and the worker who is going to work for the cure of souls must have the same outlook. We have to bear this in mind because workers today are not taking the standpoint of the Lord Jesus Christ.

In Luke 19 we find a specimen of a lost individual. "The Son of Man has come to seek and to save that which was lost" (v. 10). Notice the setting of this statement. Zacchaeus was a chief publican and as such he was possessed of many ill-gotten gains; he was a person of wealth and position, a dishonorable man, but perfectly content with his dishonor. Zacchaeus was not troubled in the tiniest degree, his whole nature towards God was frozen, no sign of life about him. In the Far North the thermometer freezes and can record nothing, and it remains frozen until the temperature alters; when the temperature alters, then the thermometer registers. This man Zacchaeus was frozen towards God, his conscience did not bother him, he was lost, quite contented, quite happy, and quite curious. When Jesus Christ came his way, the man's nature unfroze, something began to work at once.

The first thing the worker has to learn is how to bring the Lord Jesus Christ in contact with frozen souls, those who are dead towards God, whose consciences are not the slightest bit disturbed. How is the worker to bring the Lord Jesus Christ across the life that is dead in trespasses and sins and does not know it? By the Holy Spirit and personal experience alone. By personal experience I mean what we have already insisted on: I must know personally what God has done in my soul through Jesus Christ, and I must have learned how to rely on the Holy Spirit because the Holy Spirit makes Jesus Christ present to all kinds and conditions of people. The majority of people, when they come across a nature like Zacchaeus will say that person is simply selfish, sordid, and indifferent, not convicted of sin, and it is no use to try and deal with such a person. That is the attitude we all maintain to the Zacchaeus type of person until we learn how to bring Jesus Christ close to such. Whoever Jesus Christ came across in His day, they knew where they were, and they either rebelled or followed Him. They either went away exceedingly sorrowful, or they turned with their whole nature toward Him.

The next thing we have to learn by contact with Jesus Christ is this, that if the whole human race—everybody, good, bad, and indifferent—is lost, we must have the boundless confidence of Jesus Christ Himself about us; we must know that He can save anybody and everybody. There is a great deal of importance to be attached to this point. Just reflect in your mind and think of some lives you know that are frozen; there is no conviction of sin; they are dishonorable, and they know it; they are abnormal, off the main track altogether, but they are not a bit troubled about it; talk to them about their wrongdoing and they are totally indifferent. You have to learn how to introduce the atmosphere of the Lord Jesus Christ around those souls. As soon as you do, something happens. Look what happened to Zacchaeus—"And Zacchaeus stood and said to the Lord, 'Look, Lord, I give half of my goods to the poor; and if I have taken anything from anyone by false accusation, I restore fourfold.' " (Luke 19:8). Who had been talking to him about his doings? Not a soul. Jesus had never said a word about his evil doings. What awakened him? What suddenly made him know where he was? The presence of Jesus!

Wherever a worker for God goes the same thing will happen if the Spirit of God is getting His way through that man or woman. If you are right with God in personal experience, saved and sanctified (to use our own technical words), and the Spirit of God is getting His way with you, other people will get to know where they are wrong, and until they learn the reason they will say you are criticizing them; but you are perfectly conscious that you have never criticized them. What has happened? This very thing: the Holy Spirit's presence through you has brought the atmosphere that Jesus Christ's presence always brought, and has thawed the ice around their minds and their consciences and they are beginning to be convicted.

Let me insist that the worker must know how to bring every kind and condition of person into contact with Jesus Christ, and the only way that can be done is by reliance on the Holy Spirit and by personal experience. If you are trying to work for God and have no definite experience of your own and do not know how to rely on the Holy Spirit, God grant that you may come to the place where you do know; then wherever you go the atmosphere produced will thaw things around people's consciences and hearts.

People's minds will always assent that Jesus Christ is right—why? Because Jesus Christ is Incarnate Reason. There is something in Jesus Christ that appeals to everyone, no matter what condition he or she is in. If Jesus Christ is brought into contact with one, though that one seem to us dead and indifferent, destitute of anything like goodness—let that person come in contact with Jesus Christ by the Holy Spirit, and you will instantly see that he or she can grasp something about Him in a way we cannot understand unless we know the Holy Spirit.

Jesus Christ always appeals to people's consciences—why? Because He is Incarnate Righteousness. So many people try to explain things about Jesus Christ, but no worker need ever try to do that. You cannot explain things about Jesus Christ; rely on the Holy Spirit and He will explain Jesus to the soul. Let me recommend you to have this boundless confidence in Jesus Christ's power as you go into work for God! If you do not believe practically in your heart that the Lord Jesus Christ can alter and save the person you are talking to, you limit Jesus Christ in that life. You may say, "Oh, yes, Jesus Christ can save you; He can alter the whole thing and can put His new life within you and make you a new person." But if you do not believe He can do it, you limit God's power in that life, and God holds you responsible. So the first thing the worker must do is to keep his or her heart always believing in Jesus.

Are you in constant contact with frozen natures in your own family, in your business, in your friendships? You have talked with them, prayed with them, you have done everything you know how, but there is not the slightest sign of conviction of sin, no trouble of conscience or heart. They are not out-and-out sinners, but you know that they are in-and-in sinners; you know they are wrong and twisted and have things that are not clean, but you cannot make them realize it; they always get away, frozen and untouched. Then bring your own soul face-to-face with Jesus Christ: "Lord, do I believe that You can thaw that man's nature, that woman's nature, until the Holy Spirit has a chance of saving him or her?" That is the first difficulty to be overcome—what state of faith in Jesus Christ have I? Then next ask yourself, do I believe that the Lord Jesus Christ can take that selfish, sensual, twisted, self-satisfied nature that is all wrong and out of order—do I believe that He can make it perfect in the sight of God? Oh, do let us get back to this tremendous confidence in the Lord Jesus Christ's power! Back to reliance on the Holy Spirit, and to remembering that Jesus came to seek the lost.

In the fifteenth chapter of Luke's gospel, our Lord spoke about the joy of finding lost things, and to me there is always this appeal: the Lord wants my eyes to look through; is He looking through them? The Lord wants my brain to think through; is He thinking through it? The Lord wants my hands to work with; is He working with them? The Lord wants my body to live and walk in for one purpose—to go after the lost from His standpoint; am I letting Him walk and live in me? The worker must see that Jesus Christ has His right of way within in each particular. Oh, the number of men and women today who are working on the line of self-realization seeking the training of the mind and of the body—for what purpose? To help them realize themselves! Jesus Christ wants our bodies so that He can work through them to find those who are out of the way. Do remember that it is the most practical thing on this earth to be a worker for the cure of souls. You have to rely on the Holy Spirit and to live among human facts and Bible facts. Have you, Christian worker, accepted the verdict of Jesus Christ regarding the human race, that all are lost, and have you got boundless confidence in Jesus Christ—are you perfectly certain that if a soul can only get in contact with Jesus, He can save that one absolutely?

I want to give one word of warning to workers for God, especially Sunday school teachers and preachers of the gospel—beware of the snare of putting anything first in your mind but Jesus Christ. If you put the needs of your people first, there is something between you and the power of God. Face Jesus Christ steadily, and allow nothing—no work and no person— to come between you and Him. For what purpose? That the Holy Spirit may flow through you in your preaching to the needs of the people around. You will find that people will always distinguish between that kind of message and the message that is spoken out of sympathy with them. There is only one Being who understands us all and that is the Holy Spirit, and He understands the Lord Jesus Christ, too; and if you keep the avenues of your soul open to Him, and get your messages from Him, and see that you allow nothing to obscure Him, you will find He will locate the people. For every new message you give, God will give you people who have been convicted by it, and you will have to deal with them whether you like it or not; and you will have not only to deal with them, but you will have to take them on your heart before God. God will make you work for the cure of the souls He has wounded by your message. If the wounding has come along His line, the line of the faithful proclamation of His message, He will let you see Him healing them through you as a worker, as you rely on the Holy Spirit. God grant that as we go forth to our varied work we may be filled with the Spirit, and then patiently do the drudgery!

I want to say one other thing that will connect this chapter with the next one—the Spirit of God will not work for the cure of some souls without you, and God is going to hold to the account of some of us the souls that have gone uncured, unhealed, untouched by Jesus Christ because we have refused to keep our souls open towards Him, and when the sensual, selfish, wrong lives came around we were not ready to present the Lord Jesus Christ to them by the power of the Holy Spirit. Workers for God, let us believe with all our hearts these divine revelations, and never despair of any soul under heaven. If you have a chronic case—I mean by that, someone who is always coming out at every altar call but is never getting anywhere, thank God for it. I have found this out, that as far as I am concerned, God uses those chronic seekers as an education to me. It is a tremendous temptation to put them on one side and say, "It is no use dealing with such people." It is! If they keep chronic long enough they will educate you so sufficiently that the Lord will be able to manifest His patience through you as He never could otherwise, and all of a sudden those souls will come into the light.

The Worker Among the Hardy Annuals

"For there are no pangs in their death, but their strength is firm" (Psalm 73:4).

By hardy annuals I mean the healthy minded sinners. We pointed out before that from Jesus Christ's point of view all are lost, but we have so narrowed and so specialized the term lost that we have missed its evangelical meaning; we have made it mean that only the people who are down— and—out in sin are lost.

In the seventeenth chapter of Acts we see Paul, the Pharisee and the sanctified apostle of God, face—to—face with healthy minded, vigorous unbelievers. Jesus Christ came in contact with such people over and over again, and you will find that you have to come in contact with them, too. They are once-born people, and perfectly content with being once-born. They are usually upright, quite sufficient for themselves morally, very bright and happy, and you seem to feel they have not the slightest need of the Lord Jesus Christ in their lives. That class formed a great setting all round our Lord's life. In the days of His flesh our Lord worked almost exclusively among Jews, but every now and again a Gentile burst through into the inner circle, and Jesus always dealt with Gentiles in a totally different manner. Whenever our Lord dealt with a religious Jew there was a serious solemnity about Him, and a serious solemnity about the Jew; but when our Lord came in contact with a Greek, He seemed to read the sharp wit of the Greek straightway and dealt with such a person accordingly.

In the fifteenth chapter of Matthew we read that our Lord departed to the region of Tyre and Sidon, the reason being that He wanted to be alone; He had had too much publicity and was trying to get His disciples away. Then a Syrophoenician woman burst through with a request to which Jesus pays no attention, the reason being quite obvious—He wanted to be quiet, and He knew perfectly well that this woman would blaze abroad more than ever what He could do. But her faith was strong, she knew that if she could get hold of the Lord Jesus He would heal her daughter. Watch how our Lord deals with her; He gives her a proverb and she gives Him back a proverb: "It is not good to take the children's bread and throw it to the little dogs."

"Yes, Lord, yet even the little dogs eat of the crumbs which fall from their masters' table" (see vv. 26–27.) Her type of mind was foreign to the religious Jews, but Jesus understood her at once, and He praised her for her faith: "O woman, great is your faith! Let it be as you desire" (v. 28).

The healthy minded tendency is very strong today. It is the explanation of Unitarianism in its shallower aspect; the explanation of the New Thought movement and the Mind Cure movement, of Christian Science; it is the explanation of how people can be quite happy, quite moral, quite upright, without having anything to do with the Lord Jesus Christ. Our Lord describes these people, in terms of the once-born, as lost. The problem for us as workers is, how are we to get these irreligious people, who are quite happy and healthy minded, to the place where they want Jesus?

The Syrophoenician woman came to our Lord at the end of a busy spell, and you will find that these healthy minded folks will often come across you when you are worn out and will ask you all kinds of questions. They did of the apostle Paul: " 'What does this babbler want to say?' . . . 'He seems to be a proclaimer of strange gods,' because he preached to them Jesus and the resurrection" (Acts 17:18). In writing to the Corinthians, Paul says, "We preach Christ crucified, . . . to the Greeks foolishness" (1 Cor. 1:23).

Every worker for God has surely come across the type of person who makes one feel foolish; the external life, and internal life as far as you know, is quite sterling and upright, and this one puts questions to you that bring you to a complete standstill; you cannot answer them, and he or she succeeds in making you feel amazingly foolish. For instance, you preach that Jesus Christ lived and died and rose again to save people from their sins and to put them right with God; these people have no sin that they are conscious of, you cannot point to a spot in their whole lives, they are healthy minded and happy, but absolutely unbelieving, and they say, "What was the use of Jesus Christ dying for me? I am all right; I do exactly what I ought to do. I am not a blackguard, I am not a thief, I am not a sinner. Why ever should Jesus Christ die for me?" Unless you are used to it that line of thing produces a sense of unutterable foolishness in you. How are we to bring the gospel of Jesus Christ, and our Lord Himself, before a man or woman of that sort?

I want us to look at three types of unbelievers—Gallio, Herod and Pilate.

Gallio was an ordinary unbeliever, upright and just, and when the apostle Paul was brought before him he did not care anything about him. "But Gallio took no notice of these things" (Acts 18:17). He said in effect, "I have nothing whatever to do with your religious quarrels, I am not here to decide questions of your law for you." The opponents of Christianity are not weak, they are opponents who are able to ignore us; so the first thing to do is to examine and see what kind of gospel we are preaching. If you are only preaching before this kind of unbeliever—upright, righteous, and just, but without a spark of religion within—that Jesus Christ can save sinners, that is not the Jesus Christ this person needs. You have to preach the Lord Jesus Christ revealed in God's Word.

The first thing I want to impress on your hearts and minds as workers is this—we must not preach one phase of Christ's work. Jesus said, "I, if I am lifted up from the earth, will draw all peoples to Myself" (John 12:32). Have I a pet doctrine I am lifting up? If I have, then these healthy minded people will simply heap ridicule on me; but when I preach Christ, something happens—the Spirit of God begins to work where I cannot. The first point for us to remember, then, is that we must preach Christ, not pet theories of our own, no matter how right and true they are, no matter how important a doctrine or how real the outcome of our Lord's work; that is not what we have to present. We have to present Jesus Christ. "Then Philip . . . preached Jesus to him" (Acts 8:35).

Paul was able to stand the ridicule, the cultured ridicule of the Athenian philosophers, because he knew Jesus Christ; he knew Him as the greatest, grandest and most worthy Being that was ever on this earth. See that you present the Lord Jesus Christ Himself to your ordinary unbeliever. The Spirit of God will guide you, as you rely on Him, to the presentation that is required for each one. Some people present Jesus Christ in packets: they have one packet of verses marked Salvation, another marked Sanctification, another marked The Baptism with the Holy Spirit. The reason they do this is easy to understand—these particular verses have been used mightily in their experience in saving souls; but as we pointed out at the first, when we begin to depend on our special prescription the Spirit of God will depart from us. In every case we have to deal with, whether it be the case of one with a frozen conscience, or a healthy minded unbeliever, we have to learn how to rely on the Holy Spirit straightway—"Lord, this person is healthy, the sense of justice clear, the record clean, but this person cares for none of these things; I cannot deal with this one." We have to present Jesus Christ in all His power, and rely on the Holy Spirit to deal with every person.

There is another type of unbeliever represented by Herod. Herod is a rare type: he was obscene; he was bad, unmentionably bad, and you will find that when he saw Jesus Christ face–to–face he was not the slightest bit troubled. Why? He had heard the voice of God before through John the Baptist, and he had ordered that voice to be silent. Herod is the presentation of the awful possibility of a fixed character, absolutely fixed in immorality. Jesus Christ did not awaken one tremor of conscience in him; he signed his own death warrant. When the voice of God came to him in repeated warnings through John the Baptist about the thing that was wrong in his life, he would not listen, he persisted in his badness until he killed all his affinity for God, and when Jesus Christ stood before him he was not an atom troubled. Did you ever notice what is recorded? "Now when Herod saw Jesus, he was exceedingly glad" (Luke 23:8)—why? For the same reason that people go to a picture show—they want to see things. We read that Herod questioned Jesus in many words; "but He answered him nothing" (v. 9). "There is sin leading to death" (1 John 5:16)—there is a final apostasy from God, there is a sealed doom on an immortal soul while it lives, where God Almighty cannot awaken one echo of response—"I do not say that he shall pray for it," said John (1 John 5:16).

If you have never faced the question yourself, face it now—you are not as bothered now as you once were, if you are bothered at all, about Jesus Christ's line of things, and you are to blame; there will come a time when you will not be bothered even as much as you are now. Once Herod heard John the Baptist gladly (See Mark 6:20). If God has ever pointed out to you in the past the one thing that is wrong in your life, you are to blame if you did not listen. A time will come when all the tremendous presentation of the truth of God will become a farce. God forbid that any worker should ever stand face—to—face with a child of perdition, with a man or woman who has apostatized from God. There is such a thing as fixity of character, and when one's prayers go out for such a one they are arrested by God, not by the devil, and frozen before they get out of the lips. This is a truth, an awful and terrible truth, but one that people will not listen to.

Another type of unbeliever is Pilate. Pilate represents the type of unbeliever who always seeks his own interests; that type is known to us all today. People belong to certain churches because it is better for their business; or they shift their membership to other churches because it is more convenient for business. A once-born individual, who acts from this point of view, is an opportunist. "If it is Jesus Christ's gospel that is in the ascendancy, then I will use it to serve my own ends." You have to bring that person face—to—face with Christ, not with your experience, but with Jesus Christ Himself.

Gallio is a type of the ordinary unbeliever, healthy minded, vigorous, strong, and happy. Is it right to be healthy minded? Of course it is. Is it right to be happy? Of course it is. That is why the new phases of thought we have alluded to are spreading and putting down Christianity. If you can teach people how to ignore sin, you have them. If you can tell them how to ignore pain successfully, and disease and trouble, they will listen to you. If you can tell them how to ignore the possibility of judgment coming for wrongdoing, they will listen to you. If you can show people how to be delivered from the torture of sin, delivered from pain-stricken bodies, loosened from their bad pasts, then you have them. Mark you, every one of these points is right; the prince of this world delivers on that line, and so does the Lord Jesus Christ. Watch Jesus Christ's life—the people would take all His blessings, but they would not get rightly related to Him; and our difficulty is in presenting Jesus Christ apart from what He can do. How does Jesus Christ teach one to forget sin? By forgiving that one. How does an unbeliever teach one to forget sin? "Ignore it, think no more about it, realize yourself!" Can it be done? Of course it can be done. If you will just sin long enough, you will forget how sinful you are, and is it likely that if you have forgotten how wrong you have been you are going to be willing to face Jesus Christ, who, as soon as He sees you, will flash through you your past wrong? The first thing Jesus Christ does is to open one's eyes wide to the wrong and then deliver one from it. If anyone here is getting to the place of forgetting sin by ignoring it, the place of healthy mindedness and happiness without facing the past wrong, that is the characteristic of the unbeliever; but Jesus will open our eyes wide to see the wrong and will deliver us from it by putting us on another platform.

The Syrophoenician woman wanted the Lord Jesus Christ. She did not care one iota about the disciples; what she wanted was the Lord Jesus Christ. Again we read that certain Greeks came to the disciples saying, "Sir, we wish to see Jesus" (John 12:21). What did those disciples do? They went and told Jesus. Christian worker, when people belonging to the healthy unbeliever type comes to your meeting, whose presence there means "We would see Jesus," what do you do? Try and persuade them? You never will. Remember what Philip and Andrew did—they went and told Jesus. Whenever you get the request, either by presence or by word: "We would see Jesus," don't begin with "firstly, secondly, and thirdly," go to Jesus and say, "Lord, these people want to see You."

Again we come back to our first points—rely on the Holy Spirit as the most practical Being you ever knew, and live among the facts of God's Word and among human facts, and people will recognize Jesus Christ through you. God grant that every worker may ever remember that the only One who can touch the hardy annuals—whom no truth seems to upset, who carry bright, cheerful faces, and no adversity turns them aside—is the Lord Jesus Christ Himself. People say that it is so hard to bring Jesus Christ and present Him before the lives of people today. Of course it is, it is so hard that it is impossible except by the power of the indwelling Holy Spirit. A crisis comes in everyone's life. The 107th Psalm is a record of people who would not come to God until they were at their wits' end. When they were at their wits' end, then they cried to God and He heard them.

If you go and tell people it is better to be good than bad, they will say, "Yes, that is so, but how are you going to make bad people good?" That is the problem. Unless your religion will go to the lowest and the worst and the most desperate case you know of, your religion is of no use. There are a great many forms of belief which cannot begin to touch the worst of humankind; they can only deal with cultured minds and hearts. Jesus Christ's religion goes down to the lowest of the low as well as up to the highest of the high, and to all in between. The marvel of Jesus Christ is that He takes facts as they are. He Himself is the answer to every problem of heart and mind and life. The next time you come across a hardy annual, see that you lay hold of God for that one until Jesus Christ is presented by the power of the Holy Spirit, and then you will see the altered face, the altered attitude, and the altered life.

The Worker Among Backsliders

"And on some have mercy with fear; hating even the garment spotted by the flesh" (Jude 23).

The best example of a backslider in the New Testament (the word backslider is never used in the New Testament, it is an Old Testament word) is in 2 Tim. 4:10, "For Demas has forsaken me, having loved this present world"—he has gone back to where he prefers. Couple with that Jer. 2:13 and you will have a good indication of what a backslider is: "For My people have committed two evils: they have forsaken Me, the fountain of living waters, and hewn themselves cisterns—broken cisterns that can hold no water." Backsliding is twofold, and the term can only be applied to people in this condition. We use the word very loosely, we apply it to people who are degenerating, to people who have committed sin; but a backslider is neither one nor the other, a backslider is worse than both. He is worse than a person who is degenerating, and worse than a person who has committed sin; he has forsaken God and taken up with something else.

It is customary to talk of Peter as being a backslider when he denied his Lord; what happened to Peter was that he got a revelation of what he was capable of, of denying his Lord with oaths and curses. What were the conditions that led to Peter's fall? He had followed Jesus out of genuine devotion, and in true loyalty of heart to Jesus he had pictured a great many things that might happen, but never in his wildest moment did he imagine that Jesus Christ was tamely going to give Himself up to the powers of the world. When Peter saw Jesus Christ quietly give Himself right over to the rabble and let them take Him, all Peter's thoughts were turned into confusion, his heart was in despair, and in that condition, he "followed Him at a distance" (Matt. 26:58).

Then when he was tormented by stinging questions, he suddenly found in himself this awful condition he was totally ignorant of, a condition that made him deny with oaths and curses that he ever knew Jesus. Remember, Peter belonged to a dispensation we cannot begin to imagine, a dispensation before Jesus Christ died and rose again; but if we do not live in the dispensation Peter lived in, we can understand the people he represents. Peter was loyal hearted and devoted to Jesus, but grossly ignorant of what he was capable of—quite loyal, but quite ignorant—and in the trying crisis, suddenly, to his amazement, he found that he was capable of evil that horrified him.

The way God deals with a backslider, and teaches us to deal with a backslider, is clear enough for us to talk about it now.

Let us first of all examine for ourselves and find out whether in using the word backslider we are applying it to the right condition of a person. The backslidden condition is twofold: It is forsaking God and taking up with something else; it is not the condition of awakening to the presence of the disposition of sin in one's self. A backslider does know what God's grace is, does know what sin is, and does know what deliverance is, but has deliberately forsaken God and gone back because he or she loved something else better.

The question is often asked, "Can Christians sin?" Certainly, but the sin must be confessed immediately and forgiven, for if Christians allow an act of sin to go on it will lead steadily on until they will pervert all the ways of God and hew out ways for themselves.

The statement is frequently made that in dealing with a backslider, the worker has to bring that one to being born again of the Spirit. A backslider does not have to be born again, but is in a much worse condition than someone not born again: the backslidings have to be healed and restored. The statements in the Bible about backsliding are very solemn. Backsliding is the most awful crime spiritually; it is forsaking God and hewing out for one's self "broken cisterns that can hold no water." With a backslider it is not the question of a soul needing to be born again, but a much harder case than one who has never been born again. Do not get confused because when you have to face backsliders you find you cannot deal with them as you deal with any ordinary sinners. Their hearts are frozen, they are not convicted of sin, they are absolutely dull and dead toward all God wants. They will tell you quite mechanically, "Oh yes, I once knew God, I did experience this and that, but I deliberately stepped aside." The process may be gradual, but the backsliding condition is reached by forsaking God and taking up with something else.

In 2 Peter 2:15 you will find a luminous word for workers—"They have forsaken the right way and gone astray, following the way of Balaam the son of Beor, who loved the wages of unrighteousness." Who was Balaam? A prophet. What was his way? Making a market of his gift. The New Testament speaks in three different ways about Balaam: "the way of Balaam," "the error of Balaam" (Jude 11) and "the doctrine of Balaam" (Rev. 2:14). The way of Balaam is to make a market of one's gift, presuming on it, putting one's self in God's showroom. "I am here as a specimen of what God can do." When Christians begin to put themselves into the "show business," that is the way towards backsliding. The error of Balaam is seeing only the standard of natural morality and never discerning God's ways behind. When a Christian gets into the way of following his or her own wise, commonsense morality rather than the dictates of the Spirit of God backing the Word of God, that one is on the high road to backsliding. Beware how you guide your Christian life and your Christian experience. Are you simply taking the ordinary high standards of the world in your business? Beware, that is an error that leads to backsliding. "Oh, well, they all do it, I must do the same." That is the ordinary standard; if it conflicts in the tiniest degree with the clear standard of God, beware! It is an error that leads to the false doctrine which is the very heart of backsliding, making a judicious mixup between corrupt worldliness, and godliness. That is the way backsliding will begin; it is fixing your eyes on the wrong thing. The doctrine of Balaam is the corrupting of God's people. Balaam taught Balak to corrupt the people by enticing them to marry the women of Moab. That is the Old Testament incident, but what does it mean? It means trying to compromise between corrupt worldliness and Christian profession.

These are three dangerous characteristics pointed out in the New Testament, and they are fruitful in backsliding.

When you come to deal with backsliders, one of the greatest dangers is that they spread their disease more quickly than any other. The presence of one backslider is a peril to a whole community. His or her influence is ten times worse than a hundred sinners who have never been saved, and the worker for God who begins to deal with a backslider has to learn, first of all, one's unutterable powerlessness to touch such a person.

Let us face the backslider now. Are you going to begin by asking one to receive the Spirit of God? You will have no answer. One may say, "Yes, Lord, I am sorry, please give me the Holy Spirit," but God won't. You won't find one case anywhere on record in the Old or New Testament in which God deals with a backslider along those lines. Let me take as an illustration the parable in the fifteenth chapter of Luke. I know this parable is used in many ways, but I want to use it as a picture of the backslider. It is obvious why it is called The Parable of the Prodigal Son, but it is not called so in the Bible; it is called The

Parable of the Two Sons. One son went away and spent his substance in riotous living, the other son stayed at home. Each is as bad as the other. The spirit of the stay-at-home was every bit as bad as the wild riot of the younger boy who went away.

Did the father send any message to the far country after the younger boy? There is no record of any message being sent. What did the younger boy have to do? He had to do exactly what is recorded in Hosea long before that picture was painted by our Lord—he had to return. Drawn by God? It does not say so. Read the fourteenth chapter of Hosea: "I will heal their backsliding" (v. 14); but the backslider has to get up first, leave the pigs and what pigs eat, and go back to where he came from. Help granted him? None whatever. Messages from the home country? Not one. Tender touches of God's grace on his life? No. Can you picture that prodigal son returning, a degraded, sunken, sin-stained person, going back in all the cruel, bald daylight? Oh, it is a hard way to go back out of a backslider's hell; a hard, hard way! Every step of it is cruel, every moment is torture. But what happened? Before that younger son had got very far, the father saw him "and ran and fell on his neck and kissed him" (Luke 15:20)!

Worker for God among backslidden souls, remember God's way, put the sting, if you can, into the backslider's soul, that he or she may get up and come back to God. And what has that one to do? Take words and say, "By my iniquity I have fallen" (see Hos. 14:1). Did the prodigal son take with him words? He did, he rehearsed them over and over again where he was among the pigs "I will say to my father this and that," he had it all by heart. Does Hosea say the same? He does: "Take words with you, and return to the Lord. Say to Him, 'Take away all iniquity' " (14:2). What does iniquity mean? Unequal dealing, turning out of the way.

Is there a backslider listening to this? Then rouse yourself and go back to God. "But I feel no drawing." You won't feel any. I do not find one instance in the Bible of God drawing a backslider in the same way that He draws a sinner. The word to the backslider is: Return. "Take words with you, and return to the Lord. Say to Him, 'Take away all iniquity.' "

Every Christian worker will bear me out in this next statement, that in dealing with a backslider, you are exhausted to the last drop of your energy. When we work with other classes, like those we have been touching on, God seems to supply grace at the very moment; but we need to remember that if in the other cases we need to rely on the Holy Spirit, we need to do so here a thousand times more. Intercessory prayer for a backslider is a most instructive but a most trying work for God, and it will teach the worker that prayer is not only making petitions, but that prayer is breathing an atmosphere. The Christian church nearly always separates those two; when it emphasizes the atmosphere of prayer, it forgets the petition; and when it emphasizes the petition it is apt to forget the atmosphere, but the two must go together, and you need to be freshly bathed moment by moment in the limpid life of God (if I may use the phrase) as you pray for your backslider. If ever the worker needs "the wisdom that is from above" (James 3:17), it is in the moment of dealing with a backslider. How am I going to awaken, how am I going to sting into action, a backslidden soul? How am I going to get that soul to go back?

I said just now that no message was sent to the far country; God sends none, but, worker for God, will you be a message from the Father? Will you so bathe your life in the atmosphere of prayer that when you come in contact with a backslidden soul, it will awaken a remembrance of the Father, awaken a remembrance of what that soul once was? Will you let your life be like a bunch of flowers from the Father's home garden, just awakening for one moment a remembrance of what life once was, and then pass on, and pray and watch, and you will be mightily rewarded by God when you see that poor backslidden soul get up and go back to God, taking words and saying, "By my iniquity I have fallen."

If ever you hear a testimony along this line, "I was a backslider, but, thank God, I am healed now," do call a halt in that soul. Backsliding in the Bible is called by words used for the most shocking immorality. Can you imagine anybody who has been guilty of an awful moral crime talking about it in the glib, offhand way some people talk about backsliding? When a backslider has been reclaimed by God and brought back, when he or she has returned and has been met by God, the memory of the past is too tremendously humiliating to be mentioned often, and when it is mentioned the atmosphere of the life is one of deep repentance towards God. Never sympathize with a backslider; do all in your power to goad that one to return to God. If you cannot do it in words, do it by living in the atmosphere of God and awakening some remembrance of what he or she once was.

Another illustration of backsliding is in the twenty-third chapter of Matthew. It is not in reference to a person, but to the city of Jerusalem, but it gives a good picture of the way God deals with backsliders: "O Jerusalem, Jerusalem, the one who kills the prophets and stones those who are sent to her! How often I wanted to gather your children together, as a hen gathers her chicks under her wings, but you were not willing! See! Your house is left to you desolate; for I say to you, you shall see Me no more till you say, 'Blessed is He that comes in the name of the Lord!' " (vv. 37–39). "How often I wanted . . . but you were not willing!"

Oh, if any here should be backsliders, let me counsel you to return to God, and tell Him that you have fallen away from Him by your own unequal doings. Take with you words and tell Him so; let the lash fall, and before you know another thing God will receive you! The prodigal son was all but choked on the bosom of his father before he got half his recital out; but he had to show that he was in earnest, he had to return first, and you must do the same.

Christian worker, if you have someone in your mind who is a backslider, one who did know the grace of God, who did run well but who has compromised, has a name to live but is dead, then God grant you may realize the filling up of "what is lacking in the afflictions of Christ" (Col. 1:24), in intercessory prayer. The backsliders are the most dangerous class under heaven to touch, and no one but a man or woman who knows how to live bathed moment by moment in the love of God, who knows how to prevail in prayer, ought to touch the case of a backslider. It needs the wisdom that comes from above, and if you have indeed been led by God to face such a life, do it on God's line. Do not try and bring God around by way of your ignorance; go along the clearly discerned lines that are given in His Word. Get that one to understand, either through his or her own intelligence or by praying, that one must return of one's own accord.

"Take words with you, and return to the Lord." Then God says, "I will heal their backsliding, I will love them freely."

The Worker Among
the Two-Faced

"Even so you also outwardly appear righteous to men, but inside you are full of hypocrisy and lawlessness" (Matthew 23:28).

By two-faced I do not mean the kind of character John Bunyan refers to in his Mr. Facing-both-ways, I mean a person guilty of internal hypocrisy. Two-faced is simply a figure of speech for double dealing and falsehood. If you never have taken the trouble to go through the Bible to see how much God's Word has to say about the two-faced, do it, and you will be surprised. Let me give you one or two passages to show you that this subject is not isolated or novel, not something taken because it sounds different from what is usually taken. It is taken because it describes a class of people who are so difficult to deal with that we rarely hear them mentioned.

"Beware of false prophets, who come to you in sheep's clothing, but inwardly they are ravenous wolves" (Matt. 7:15).

"For false christs and false prophets will rise and show great signs and wonders to deceive, if possible, even the elect" (Matt. 24:24).

"Having a form of godliness, but denying its power. And from such people turn away! For of this sort are those who creep into households and make captives of gullible women loaded down with sins, led away by various lusts" (2 Tim. 3:5−6.)

These are simply a few of a number of passages in the Bible where the Spirit of God and our Lord draw the portrait of the two-faced. Let me repeat it, the two-faced are the hardest and most difficult people to work among. When we face the double-dealing, two-faced people of God our hearts sink, our whole souls are terrified. We must not read the Bible like children. God requires us to read it as men and women, spiritual men and women, I mean. There are things in the Bible that stagger us, things that amaze and terrify; and the worker for God needs to understand not only the terrors of life around, but the terrors of life as God's Book reveals it.

Let us go back to the incident recorded in 2 Sam. 12. For subtlety, for amazing insight and sublime courage, Nathan is unequaled; and what a soul was David to have in his list for God! Would to God there were more preachers and Christian workers after the stamp of Nathan. David did not even begin to realize, after a year of the grossest and most dastardly hypocrisy, that Nathan was brandishing the sword straight into his own conscience, and only when David had made his answer and Nathan had heaved out the strong denunciations of God and thrust the sword straight home with, "You are the man!" (2 Sam. 12:7) did David say, "I have sinned against the Lord" (v. 13). There was no bungling about Nathan's work.

If you want to know how it was possible for a mighty saint of God like David to have sinned the most wicked sin possible—I do not refer to adultery or to murder, but to something infinitely worse: a deep, subtle, inward hypocrisy, tremendous and profound; David lived it for a year and administered justice while all the time he was a "whitewashed tomb"(see Matt. 23:27). You must first allow God to examine deep down into the possibilities of your own nature.

Mark how Nathan came to David. "And the Lord sent Nathan to David" (2 Sam. 12:1). Be sure, before you face the hypocrite and the two-faced soul, that God has sent you, and then use all the subtlety you have from the knowledge of your own heart. Any worker who has stood before God's all-searching eye for five minutes is not staggered at David's fall. Any heart sin recorded is possible for any human heart, and why I say that the worker among the two-faced will find the hardest work is to get subtlety, wisdom, not only from God on High, but from a strange, mighty probing of one's own nature. If the worker for God is going to go all lengths for God for the cure of souls, one has to allow God to examine deep down the possibilities of one's own nature. That is why it is hard to deal with the two-faced. That is why, Christian worker, God will take you through disciplines and experiences that are not meant for your particular life; they are meant to make you ready for God to send as He sent Nathan. Then you can use that subtle sword. "Therefore be wise as serpents and harmless as doves" (Matt. 10:16), said our Lord.

One solid year of deep heart hypocrisy in King David's life, suddenly faced by Nathan, and watch how Nathan dealt with it. He used a parable of such God-given insight that David was blind as to his meaning. The sword went straight into David's conscience. As soon as David said, "The man who has done this shall surely die" (2 Sam. 12:5)—"he is worthy of this and it shall be done," instantly, with sublime courage, Nathan said, "You are the man!" Then came the denunciations of God.

Worker for God, before you go among the infirm, the sick, the subtle, the hypocritical, let God deal with you. A child cannot wield the sword of the Spirit; it must be wielded by one fed on strong meat, one who has been deeply dealt with and examined by God's Spirit, in whom the last springs and possibilities of iniquity and wrong in the worker's own nature have been disclosed, that he or she may understand the marvel of God's grace.

Notice what the apostle Paul did in a similar case. Read his Epistle to the Galatians, and see how he dealt with false brethren—"And this occurred because of false brethren secretly brought in (who came in by stealth to spy out our liberty which we have in Christ Jesus, that they might bring us into bondage), to whom we did not yield submission even for an hour, that the truth of the gospel might continue with you" (2:4–5), "False brethren"—mark the phrase, it is not mine, it is Paul's; they were brethren, though two-faced and untrue. What are we to do with them? "To whom we did not yield submission even for an hour"—why? That our views might be expounded? No. That they might be detected as hypocrites? No. "That the truth of the gospel might continue with you." "Let brotherly love continue" (Heb. 13:1). This is perfect love to God; blazing, fiery zeal for God's honor, and mercilessness against God's enemies. There is a time to smite and a time to smile; a time to slay and thrust straight home when the true, sterling worth of your own repentance and the true, sterling worth of God's work of grace in your heart is put to the test.

When these false brethren crept in secretly, cunningly and craftily working against the honor of the Lord Jesus Christ, how did Paul deal with them? He withstood them; but be careful when you deal with false brethren that you are on the apostle's line. If you dare to touch a false brother and your life has not been riddled through by God's searchlight, beware! If you are going to face false brethren, if you are going to work for the cure of the two-faced souls, if you are going to work so that the thrust of the sword of the Spirit will go straight home to the conscience, be prepared first to be dealt with by God, or else, if you begin to use your suspicions, your carping criticisms instead of God's insight, you may get a reply like this: "Jesus I know, and Paul I know, but who are you?" (Acts 19:15).

Set a thief to catch a thief, that is the method of the world; but when God Almighty sends a worker He sends one whom He has literally turned inside out, in a spiritual sense, one whose disposition He has altered and allowed the man or woman to know what He has done. There is no false knowledge in that worker's life. That worker goes straight for one purpose, the condemnation of the sinner, not to show one's own discernment, but to bring the soul out of its duplicity, out of its hypocrisy, into the light of God. Don't begin to work from your carnal suspicions. How many people mistake carnal suspicions for spiritual discernment! If God gives you a spirit of discernment, it is all right, there are times when He does, but I would like to warn you—never ask God to give you discernment. I have heard people ask God to give them the spirit of discernment, and I have felt constrained to say, "Lord, do not lead that soul into temptation."

If God is going to give you power, Christian worker, to work for the cure of souls in their worst form, among the two-faced and the hypocritical, remember, first He will give you such an insight into the possibilities of your own sinfulness, and then such a comprehension of the marvels of His grace and wonderful salvation that you will have all the subtlety Nathan had. You will not be silent, you will speak out. Oh, for more voices to speak out when false doctrines are being taught! Would there were more to stand on the Nathan line, and wield the sword with all the wisdom of God's Spirit into the consciences of people, so that before they could know what they were driving at, the sword would have gone straight home with a "You are the man!" Oh, for more of that kind of wisdom! To be right with God, so examined by God, that God can send the blade of the anecdote, or the blade of the parable, straight to the imagination, and while the imagination is busy the sword has gone straight home. Then comes the application without a moment's delay—"You are the man!" and the cry goes up, "I have sinned against the Lord." Then listen to Nathan's message to David afterwards: "And Nathan said to David, 'The Lord also has put away your sin; you shall not die' "(2 Sam. 12:13). What a message!

One more thing, in the multitude of all the talk and all the words today do not forget the first point—if you are going to work for the cure of souls, you cannot choose the kind of souls you are going to work with. And when God brings you face-to-face with a two-faced life, an inwardly hypocritical life, then you will understand what the examination of God's Spirit is in you. Then you will understand what it is to be used in God's hands as "a new threshing sledge with sharp teeth" (Isa. 41:15). Then you will know what it is for the sword of God to wound and bruise you until you can feel no more, that He may thrust home the sword that will kill the error and save the soul you are driving at. God grant we may understand that working for the cure of souls is not a babe's work; it is adult work, requiring adult power, grasped and transformed by God Almighty, so that God can get straight through the worker to the individuals He is waiting for.

The one who stands beside Nathan, in the New Testament, is John the Baptist. There was no belittling of his message; when he was before Herod there was no trimming down the message to win Herod's favor, no subtle telling a lie against himself for his own vanity. There is more of that done than most people think. Nathan and John the Baptist came straight from God, and if you come straight from God you have to be spotless; there must be nothing between you and God, Christian worker. John the Baptist came straight from God and talked straight for God. Do you talk straight for God? When the message you have to deliver, preacher, strikes straight home, don't water it down just a little. Go straight for God if you come from Him. Neither for fear nor favor alter the message. What happened to John the Baptist? He went straight back to God, minus his head. That was the result of his message.

The Spirit of God discerns more incapacity in workers in dealing with the two-faced than in any other way. God grant we may so live under His searchlight that we may come straight from God and talk straight for God. It is easier to be silent than to obey God when you are face-to-face with a hypocrite, and if you are silent, you will get the applause of others. "When I say to the wicked, 'You shall surely die,' and you give him no warning, nor speak to warn the wicked from his wicked way, to save his life, that same wicked man shall die in his iniquity; but his blood I will require at your hand" (Ezek. 3:18).

The next time you take a meeting there may be a person after God's own heart there, but he or she has got on the line of internal hypocrisy and so may end at perdition: you be faithful! You may have added to your list that day the soul of a David. But if you, seeing and knowing this person, begin to trim your message, God will require that one's blood at your hands. "If you warn the wicked, and he does not turn from his wickedness, nor from his wicked way, he shall die in his iniquity; but you have delivered your soul" (Ezek. 3:19). Obey God at every price! But mark you, Christian worker, if you obey God, He is going to let you be tried to the point of agony. In dealing with souls, it is easy to dabble in shallow water with the abnormal, it is easy to dabble with the lost, it is easy to dabble with the ordinary, easily comprehended sinners, but when we begin to work with the backsliders and when we are face-to-face with the internal hypocrites, then we need the subtlety which comes through the Spirit of God, and many draw back. God grant many may go forward!

The Worker Among Sick Souls

"The destruction that lays waste at noonday"
—Psalm 91:6.

I wonder if this has been growing clear to you: that we cannot understand the cases we have to deal with. One of the first things a worker for God has to learn by experience is that strangely obvious lesson, that none of us can understand the cases we meet to work with. Then how can we work for the cure of them? Remember the first principles we laid down: By knowing Jesus Christ for ourselves experientially, and then by relying on the Holy Spirit.

"Then I hated all my labor in which I had toiled under the sun" (Eccl. 2:18). These words were written by Solomon, the wisest man who ever lived, and you will find the last summing up of all he says is the statement of a sick soul, not a healthy minded soul, not a vigorous, sunshiny, hopeful soul, but exactly the opposite.

We have spoken about the worker for the cure of souls among the hardy annuals, the hardy sinners, nothing sick about them, they are healthy and happy and wholesome. Now I want to take exactly the opposite kind of people. If our religion is only a religion of cheerfulness for the healthy minded, it is no good for London, because more than half the people there—a great deal more than half—are not able to be cheerful; their minds and consciences and bodies are so twisted and tortured that exactly the opposite seems to be their portion. All the talking and preaching about healthy mindedness, about cheering up and living in the sunshine will never touch that crowd. If all Jesus Christ can do is to tell a person to cheer up when miserable; if all the worker for God can do is to tell people they have no business to have the blues—I say if that is all Jesus Christ's religion can do, then it is a failure. But the wonder of our Lord Jesus Christ is just this: that you can face Him with any kind of men or women you like, and He can cure them and put them into a right relationship with God.

The New Testament mentions quite a few of these sick souls. We will take two just now—Thomas and Mary Magdalene.

Thomas was naturally gloomy, not happy and healthy minded; that was not the way he was made. He was loyal to Jesus Christ, but he took the sick view of life; he always thought the worst was going to happen. You remember that when Lazarus died and Jesus said He was going to Bethany, Thomas said, "Let us also go, that we may die with Him" (John 11:16). It was no use going to Thomas and preaching the gospel of cheerfulness; you cannot alter facts by saying "Cheer up." What did Jesus Christ do for Thomas? He brought him into personal contact with Himself and altered him entirely (see John 20:24–29).

Mary Magdalene was another type of the sick soul, tortured and afflicted. It was no use going to Mary and telling her to believe there was no such thing as the devil, no such thing as sin, she was absolutely incapable of taking the first step. What did Jesus Christ do for Mary Magdalene? Help her to be happy when she was miserable? Help her to realize that there was no such thing as demon possession? No. He turned out the demons and healed her (see Luke 8:2).

In the second chapter of Hebrews we read of a great crowd of sick souls who were subject to bondage through fear of death, and Jesus Christ came to deliver them from their bondage; and in 1 Corinthians 11:30 we read, "For this reason many are weak and sick among you, and many sleep." I have simply run over these cases to show that there is sufficient indication in the Book of God for us to recognize that there are naturally sick souls.

One word about the physical condition of people. There is a threshold to our nerves, that is, a place where the nerves begin to record. Some people's nerves do not record things as quickly as others. Some people have what is called the misery threshold of nerves, the threshold where the nerves begin to record is much lower down than it is in other people. Take it in connection with sound: some people can sleep in a tremendous racket, noise makes not the slightest difference to them. The ear gathers up vibrations, and only when those vibrations are quick enough do we hear. If the threshold of our hearing were lower, we would hear anything that makes waves in the atmosphere, we would hear the flowers grow, everything that grows makes a motion in the atmosphere. The majority of us have a threshold that is high up, and we cannot hear unless there is sufficient vibration in the atmosphere. Get a nervous system where the threshold of nerves is low, and life is an abject torture to that one wherever he or she goes. What is the good of telling this person to cheer up? There is a bigger problem there than we can touch. This one is in contact with forces which the majority of us know nothing about; tortured by things we never hear, tortured by things we never feel. Such people take a very gloomy view of life; they cannot help it.

When a worker meets a soul like that, what is he or she going to do—preach the gospel of temperament, "Cheer up and look on the bright side," or preach Jesus Christ? The gospel of cheerfulness is the catchword of the day—it may be all very well among people who are naturally cheerful, but what about the people who cannot be cheerful, who through no fault of their own have bodies where the threshold of their nerves is so low down that life is a misery? Read the second chapter of Hebrews again, and you will find it says that Jesus Christ took on Him not the nature of angels, but, "Inasmuch then as the children have partaken of flesh and blood, He Himself likewise shared in the same" (v. 14). Jesus Christ took on Him a flesh and blood nature with nerves and He knows exactly how the human frame is tuned and how it is tortured. Every Christian worker ought to know how to bring the sick souls, the souls that take the gloomy view, to Jesus Christ. These people will accept all you say about the need to receive His Spirit, but nothing happens; they do not cheer up. How are we going to bring Jesus Christ into contact with them?

If you read Acts 10:38 you will find Peter says a wonderful thing about "how God anointed Jesus of Nazareth with the Holy Spirit and with power, who went about doing good and healing all who were oppressed by the devil." Peter had just awakened to the fact that "God shows no partiality" (v. 34), and it is important to notice that he says God anointed Jesus of Nazareth with the Holy Spirit and with power. Peter had never preached like that before. When he preached to the Jews he had presented Jesus Christ as being, first, the Son of God. As soon as he came in contact with the outside crowd who were not Jews, who were not religious, the Spirit of God made him present Him as Jesus of Nazareth. When people are being led of the Spirit of God, they never preach their convictions.

But I want to notice what it was Peter said Jesus of Nazareth did; He healed "all who were oppressed by the devil." There are only two religions that accept gloom as a fact (I mean by gloom, sin, anguish and misery, the things that make people feel that life is not worth living), Buddhism and Christianity. Every other religion ignores it. This is the age of the gospel of cheerfulness. We are told to ignore sin, ignore the gloomy people, and yet more than half the human race is gloomy. Sum up your own circle of acquaintances, and then draw your inference. Go over the list, and before long you will have come across one who is gloomy, one who has a sick view of things, and you cannot alter that one. How are you going to get that oppression taken off? Tell this person to take so many weeks holiday by the sea? Take iron pills and tonics? No! Living in the peace and joy of God's forgiveness and favor is the only thing that will brighten up and bring cheerfulness to such a one. Only when God takes a life in hand can there come deliverance from the blues, deliverance from fits of depression, discouragement, and all such moods. The Scriptures are full of admonitions to rejoice, to praise God, to sing aloud for joy; but only when one has a cause to rejoice, to praise, and to sing aloud, can these things truly be done from the heart. In the physical realm the average sick patient does not take a very bright view of life, and with the sick in soul true brightness and cheer are an impossibility. Until the soul is cured there is always an underlying dread and fear which steals away the gladness and the "joy inexpressible and full of glory" (1 Peter 1:8), which God wishes to be the portion of all His children.

In dealing with sick souls, we must remember the Master's way, how He went to the root of the matter. Hear Him as He said, time and again when one was brought to Him for physical healing, "Your sins are forgiven" (Matt. 9:2; Luke 7:48). Dig out the "root of bitterness" (Heb. 12:15), then there can be no fruit to sour the life and set the nerves on edge.

My brother or sister, if you are a worker for Jesus Christ He will open your eyes wide to the fact that sin and misery and anguish are not imaginary, they are real. Anguish is as real as joy; fired, jangled, and tortured nerves are as real as nerves in order. Low threshold nerves, where everything is an exquisite misery, are as real as high threshold nerves where nothing is misery. Listen to this, they are Luther's own words:

> "I am utterly weary of life. I pray the Lord will come forthwith and carry me hence. Let Him come above all with His last judgment. I will stretch out my

neck, the thunder will burst forth and I shall be at rest." And having a necklace of white agates in his hand at the time, he added: "O God, grant that it may come without delay. I would readily eat up this necklace today for the judgment to come tomorrow."

The Electress Dowager one day, when Luther was dining with her, said to him, "Doctor, I wish you may live forty years to come."

"Madame," replied he, "rather than live forty years more, I would give up my chance of Paradise."

That was Luther speaking at the end of his life. What produced the misery? He saw the havoc the Reformation had wrought, he did not see the good, he was too near it.

There was the same thing in Goethe's writings; in 1824 he wrote:

I will say nothing against the course of my existence, but at the bottom it has been nothing but pain and burden, and I can affirm that, during the whole of my seventy-five years, I have not had four weeks of genuine well-being. It has been the perpetual rolling of a rock that must be raised up again.

Robert Louis Stevenson said that three hours out of every five he was insane with misery. John Stuart Mill said that life was not worth living after you were a boy.

This is not fiction, these are human facts. What does Christian Science do—ignores them! New Thought—ignores them! Mind Cure—ignores them! Jesus Christ opens our eyes to these facts, but here comes the difficulty: how am I to get Jesus Christ in contact with these sick souls?

In the first place, will you realize that you do not know how to do it? I want to lay that one principle down very strongly. If you think you know how to present Jesus Christ to a soul, you will never be able to do it. But if you will learn how to rely on the Holy Spirit, believing that Jesus Christ can do it, then I make bold to state that He will do it. If you get your little compartment of texts, and search them out and say, "I know how to deal with this soul," you will never be able to deal with this person; but if you realize your absolute helplessness and say, "My God, I cannot touch this life, I do not know where to begin, but I believe that You can do it," then you can do something.

It is wonderful to see Jesus Christ slip His coolness and His balm through fired and jangled nerves, turn out demons, alter the whole outlook and lift the life into a totally new relationship. Have you ever seen Him do that? I have seen Him do it twice in my lifetime, and I will never forget it. While you watch and while you realize the marvelous work of God going on in those gloomy, tortured lives, it is as if you were bathed in the sunlight of the Presence of God in a way you never are until you are face-to-face with one of these cases that make you realize your own utter helplessness, and the power of Jesus Christ.

It was Jesus Christ coming in contact with Thomas that altered his gloom; the disciples' testimony could not do it. "We have seen the Lord" (John 20:25), and out of the agony of his sick soul, Thomas said he could not, dared not, believe. "Unless I see in His hands the print of the nails, and put my finger into the print of the nails, and put my hand into His side, I will not believe." The testimony of the disciples was not the slightest bit of use, but when Jesus Christ came in contact with him, all was different. "Then He said to Thomas, 'Reach your finger here, and look at My hands; and reach your hand here, and put it into My side. Do not be unbelieving, but believing.' And Thomas answered and said to Him, 'My Lord and my God!' " (vv. 27–28).

And Mary Magdalene—what did Jesus Christ do for her? He turned the demons out of her. "Mary called Magdalene, out of whom had come seven demons" (Luke 8:2).

Demon possession means that one body can hold several personalities. Do you believe that? Very few people do today, but it is an awful fact, not only in the New Testament, but outside the New Testament, that one body may be the holder of more than one personality. How much room does thought take up? None. Personality partakes of the nature of thought. How much room does personality take up? None. "And when He stepped out on the land, there met Him a certain man from the city who had demons. . . . Jesus asked him, saying, 'What is your name?' And he said, 'Legion,' because many demons had entered him" (Luke 8:27–30). Many devils in one individual, the moderns laugh at the idea, but the poor, tortured, demon-possessed man was left alone. Jesus Christ healed him and delivered him of them all.

God grant us the grace so to rely on the Holy Spirit, so to know our ignorance, so to get out of the way with our knowledge, that we will let the Holy Spirit bring the Majestic Christ face-to-face with the diseased, sick people we meet. The majority of workers are in the road with their convictions of how God is going to work; there is no real, living, stirring, vital reliance on the Holy Spirit which places straight before the tortured, stricken soul the Mighty Lord Jesus. God grant we may so rely on the Holy Spirit that we may allow Him to introduce through the agony of our intercession—that is the point, through the agony of vicarious intercession—the Living, Mighty Christ! My brother and sister, are you willing to allow Jesus Christ to use every bit of your life to trample on in His way to another soul? Do you know anything about spending one costly drop of blood in vicarious intercession? There is nothing worked in the way of result in answer to prayer that does not cost somebody something. "Who, in the days of His flesh, when He had offered up prayers and supplications with vehement cries and tears" (Heb. 5:7). When you meet your sick soul, do you cry awhile and then go home and sleep, instead of taking that soul before God and vicariously interceding until, by reliance on the Holy Spirit, Jesus Christ is presented to that darkened, difficult life? Blessed be the Name of God, there is no case too hard for Jesus Christ!

One more thing—what produces sick souls? Our emotions are associated with certain things and the value of those things to us lies in the emotion they start. For instance, you have some things in your home that are of no use to anybody on earth, but to you they are enormously valuable. Let something come in and destroy your emotions and associations, and what kind of a world are you in? A world in which suicide is the only outlet. Let some paralysis come and destroy your emotions, all your associated ideas with things, with people, with houses, with friends, with work, and the light is gone out of the sky, the power and the joy out of life, everything is paralyzed, and the universe is one black prison. What will produce that? Look at the prodigal son. Have you ever dropped the plumb line down into his heart and tried to fathom one phase only of his cry—"I have sinned against heaven and in your sight" (Luke 15:21)? Oh, the agony of the soul that has been paralyzed on the inside—the gloom, the darkness, and the shadow! No preaching of the gospel of good cheer will touch that; it is only the great life-giving, life-imparting Christ who can touch it. Oh, my brother or sister, you have lately been brought face-to-face with some case and you have said, "This is conviction of sin," but you know it is not. You have tried all the Scriptural teaching you know, with no result. You have tried to advocate this thing and that, but no result, and you have been humiliated to the dust before God. Is not this the reason—you have been trying to find out what is wrong? God will never show you what is wrong; that is not your business. What He wants us to do is to bring the case to Him: "Lord, use my intercession as a channel through which You can reach that soul." God grant that we may be so centered in Him that He can use us in that wonderful way.

The Worker Among the Stupid Souls

"Indeed I have played the fool and erred exceedingly" (1 Samuel 26:21).

This is a statement made by the prophet of the Most High God, and a King of Israel. Before I read some passages from God's Book to show you that the stupid soul is continually brought before the attention of the reader of God's Word, I would like you to notice what the word stupid means. It does not mean ignorant, but anything formed or done without reason or judgment. Ignorance is being without knowledge, and "these times of ignorance God overlooked" (Acts 17:30). Do distinguish between ignorance and stupidity!

Let us look at one or two passages:

"And Moses and Aaron gathered the assembly together before the rock; and he said to them, 'Hear now, you rebels! Must we bring water for you out of this rock?' " (Num. 20:10).

"Because they rebelled against His Spirit, so that he spoke rashly with his lips" (Ps. 106:33).

"When anyone hears the word of the kingdom, and does not understand it, then the wicked one comes and snatches away what was sown in his heart" (Matt. 13:19).

"For we ourselves were also once foolish" (Titus 3:3).

"For of this sort are those who creep into households and make captives of gullible women loaded down with sins, led away by various lusts, always learning and never able to come to the knowledge of the truth" (2 Tim. 3:6–7).

"For though by this time you ought to be teachers, you need someone to teach you again the first principles of the oracles of God; and you have come to need milk, and not solid food" (Heb. 5:12).

My reason for running over these passages is that the truth may sink into our minds that the Bible lays a tremendous emphasis on the fact that there are stupid souls.

Now let us get back to Saul. I know it is not the usual way of summing up Saul, but I want to take him as an illustration of the stupid soul. Read the description of Saul in 1 Sam. 9:2: "And he had a choice and handsome son whose name was Saul. There was not a more handsome person than he among the children of Israel. From his shoulders upward he was taller than any of the people." His physique was magnificent, his bodily presence wonderful, but he was amazingly stupid. Samuel was known everywhere, he was such a mighty prophet and saint of God, but there were two people who did not know him—a man called Kish and his son Saul; they spent their time breeding asses, and knew nothing whatever about Samuel. Saul actually met Samuel and asked him if he could tell him where the seer was! How did Saul get the first inkling of who Samuel was? Through one of his father's servants. If you are a stupid soul spiritually, do get in touch with a godly servant—in touch with someone who does know the seer! And Samuel said to him, "I am the seer. . . . Tomorrow I will let you go, and will tell you all that is in your heart" (v. 19). Then we read that "God gave him another heart" (10:9). If Saul had gone on in obedience to God's Word, his life would have fulfilled God's intention; but instead of that, he is a model for all time of a stupid soul.

What are we to do when we come across stupid souls? Ignorant souls we can deal with—they need knowledge; the stupid soul does not need knowledge; the stupid soul needs to have the Word of God until he or she is worried by it. The difficulty is how the worker is to get the Word of God into its right place. Jesus Christ says the stupid soul is the one that hears the Word and does not understand it: "When anyone hears the word of the kingdom, and does not understand it" (Matt. 13:19). Does God hold one culpable for being stupid spiritually? He certainly does. Every case of stupidity recorded in the Bible is punished by God. How can I get the Word of God into a stupid soul? Read 1 Sam. 15:19, and see how Samuel dealt with Saul: "Why then did you not obey the voice of the Lord?"

Take the apostle Paul, the very same thing: "O foolish Galatians! Who has bewitched you that you should not obey the truth?" (Gal. 3:1). And our Lord's own words: "O foolish ones, and slow of heart to believe in all that the prophets have spoken!" (Luke 24:25).

This is the time, Christian worker, when you must use the Word until you get it wedged in somehow in that stupid soul, until it rankles and worries its way to the soul's salvation or destruction, and there was never a class that will drive a worker closer to God than the stupid souls; they will tax every bit of patience and endurance you have. They always pretend to want to do something, "always learning and never able to come to the knowledge of the truth"—why? They would not obey the Word they heard—that is the beginning. You remember Samuel asked Saul if he had fulfilled the word of God with regard to the Amalekites, and Saul said he had: " 'Blessed are you of the Lord! I have performed the commandment of the Lord.' But Samuel said, 'What then is this bleating of the sheep in my ears, and the lowing of the oxen which I hear?' " Pretending, that is the first characteristic of the stupid soul. Again, in Saul's last agony when he went off on the spiritualistic line, Samuel says the same thing: "Because you did not obey the voice of the Lord" (1 Sam. 28:18).

You will come across the stupid soul in connection with the elementary work of grace, the new birth: "I want to be sanctified,

I have done this and that and the other." Well, be perfectly certain they have not; if those things had been done, there would be no "bleating of the sheep," no provision for the lusts of the flesh, none of the laying down of careful lines for the development of things that ought not to be in the Christian life. Is any soul beginning to deceive itself? That is the danger of stupidity; when once it begins to disobey God's Word ever so little, it begins to deceive itself. "Well, God is very hard with me, I did fulfill the Word of God, I did what I knew how to." How is the worker going to get the Word of God driven straight home? As you wait before God, there is no class for which God will give you passages of Scripture more quickly than for this class, and at your peril you lower the standard of the Word of God.

The first thing I want to note with regard to the worker is this: never sympathize with a stupid soul. Sympathize with the sick soul, sympathize with the abnormal soul; sympathy is needed for nearly every soul but the stupid soul—never sympathize with stupidity in the approach of a soul to God. Watch Samuel, watch Paul, and watch our Lord—the Word of God, the Word of God, the Word of God, first, second, and last; no sympathy, no help, only the Word of God.

Have you ever noticed that if a stupid soul hears a word of God too often he or she may turn again and trample on that word? A man, who ultimately became a great power for God, on his own testimony said that the center of his life was once full of this kind of stupidity. He was a so-called worker for God for several years, until he came across this verse: "Or do you not know . . . you are not your own? For you were bought at a price" (1 Cor. 6:19–20), and he said wherever he went that verse kept chiding him; when he read a book he would come across it; when he heard a sermon it would be from that text, until he said, "At last I took my penknife and cut the verse out of every Bible I had." Then the Spirit of God awakened him as to what he had done, and he confessed the whole thing before God and God forgave him his stupidity.

Christian worker, when God gives you a word for a soul who is stupid, keep at it. This is the time when you have to keep using the verse God gives you for a soul: every time you meet, every time you write, every time you talk. The only way you will stir up that one out of stupidity is by driving home the Word of God, and presently you will see that stupid soul saved from perdition, if that one has not gone as far away from God as Saul, and as far away as many a stupid soul will go for lack of faithful workers. But if you as a worker have one strand of stupidity in you, one characteristic in your life where you are apt to make statements and judgments unreasonably, beware that your message does not become a boomerang. A boomerang is a peculiar weapon so balanced that when you fling it as far from you as you can, it comes back and hits you! God's Word is always a boomerang to the worker who uses it if he or she is not right with Him.

Worker for God, are you quite sure there is no strand of stupidity in you? Are you quite sure you are not in the category of those who are "always learning and never able to come to the knowledge of the truth"? Are you facing something about which you are very willing to be stupid? Then the Word of God in your hand will come straight back to you when you try to deal with another soul—"You are the man!" But if you are living rightly yourself, then keep on the line of pressing the Word home. Will you just run over in your mind, worker, the stupid souls you have in your Sunday school class, in your church services—are you glossing over the word God gave you for them? Hammer at it morning, noon, and night; if you cannot get at their ears, get at them by prayer. If it is Luke 11:13, then keep at it until they say, "I wish you would be quiet about Luke 11:13; is there nothing else in the Bible but that verse?" But what about "the bleating of the sheep"? That is what keeps you to your point, and God will never let you get away from it. If a person claims to have received the Spirit of God and yet has not gone on with God, there is always a word of God to tell why, and if you are a worker for God you will be a persistent annoyance and aggravation to that one whenever you meet, until ultimately he or she comes to the place of praise to God for the annoyance. Every worker can give instances of God awakening the stupid soul by persistence on the one point. This is the stern element in Christian work.

How did Jesus Christ deal with the foolishness or the stupidity of the two disciples on the road to Emmaus? These disciples were good, simple souls, honest and true, but they had become stupid, blinded by their own grief, their own point of view. What did Jesus say to them? "O foolish ones, and slow of heart to believe in all that the prophets have spoken!" The word *fool* is often used in the New Testament, but not always in the same way; here it means literally, "My little imbecile children, when will you believe all that the prophets have spoken?" This is stupidity of a totally different order, a stupidity that Jesus deals with very pointedly, but very patiently. It is a stupidity that has obliterated the interpretation of the Word of God because of personal grief and perplexity. Is Jesus Christ coming to you by the Spirit and saying, "My little imbecile child, when will you believe what I say?" Is there any particular thing in your life, Christian worker, that you have become slow of heart to believe? Do not let the stupidity grow. Get the Word of God for it. Oh, if there ever was a need, it is for people to search and ransack this Book and get at what God says. How much time have you given to finding out what the Bible has to say? An hour a day? "Oh, I cannot give an hour." Half an hour? "Oh no, I cannot give that." Five minutes? "Yes, I could do that." Well, have you done it? Five minutes a day out of twenty-four hours to find out what the Word of God says! No wonder God says, "My people do not consider" (Is. 1:3).

Never water down the Word of God to the understanding of your people. Would that God the Holy Spirit thunder that through you as He has thundered it through me! Never drag down the Word of God to anybody's understanding. Hammer at it, keep at it, and drive at it, till the laziness is taken out of people's hearts and brains and bodies, and they are willing to face what this Book has to say about their condition, and face it with the sterling earnestness they use to see what the newspapers have to say when they are on the hunt for a new job. God grant we may learn the imperativeness of getting at what the Word of God has to say about our particular need, then perhaps we will begin to understand why we have that need.

"The words that I speak to you are spirit, and they are life" (John 6:63). The Word of God is "a lamp" and "a light" (Ps. 119:105), but when people get off on the stupid lines, it is all instincts, impressions, vague ideas—"always learning and never able to come to the knowledge of the truth." Then is the time when those of reprobate mind creep in and lead astray. There are a number of creepers stealing in these days, religious creepers, and they will steal into your souls, my brother and sister, just where you are stupid. Has something been said to you recently from the Word of God that has awakened you with a startling realization to the fact that you have not obeyed God on a certain point? Then may God bring you face-to-face with a faithful worker who will bring the same thing to you, whatever it is, until you get through. When the Word of God has begun its "piercing even to the division of soul and spirit," it will have its wonder-working way and heal and recreate and dissipate the stupidity.

The Worker and the
Passion for Souls

"To the weak I became as weak, that I might win the weak. I have become all things to all men, that I may by all means save some" (1 Corinthians 9:22).

You hear people say that Paul showed his wonderful breadth of mind, his culture and generosity, his gentleness and patience, by becoming all things to all peoples. He did nothing of the sort; he said, "I have become all things to all men" for one purpose only—"that I may by all means save some." He did not say, "I became all things to all men that I might show what a wonderful being I am." There is no thought of himself in the whole matter.

The phrase a passion for souls is a dangerous one; a passion for souls may be either a diseased lust or a divine life. Let me give you a specimen of it as a diseased lust: "Woe to you, scribes and Pharisees, hypocrites! For you travel land and sea to win one proselyte, and when he is won, you make him twice as much a son of hell as yourselves" (Matt. 23:15). Proselyte is a technical word for convert, and our Lord is showing that these Pharisees had a great passion for souls which He stamped as of the devil; and if you read the thirteenth chapter of Acts you will find a remarkable thing occurred—the proselytes became exactly what Jesus Christ said they would, "twice as much a son of hell," far more superstitious and fanatical; the devout women alluded to who persecuted the apostles were proselytes (vv. 43–50). In Rev. 13:11–17, you will find again the passion for souls as a diseased lust. I refer to the beast coming up out of the earth; the consummation of his power was to get the souls of the human race into one solid mass.

But have we got clearly in our minds what the passion for souls as a divine life is? Read James 5:19–20: "Brethren, if anyone among you wanders from the truth, and someone turns him back, let him know that he who turns a sinner from the error of his way will save a soul from death and cover a multitude of sins." The apostle is talking to those whom we understand as Christians, "If anyone among you, brethren, wanders from the truth."

Again, our Lord in speaking to His disciples used some striking phrases, all of which refer to this passion for souls; in Matt. 4:18–22, He spoke about making them "fishers of men"; in John 21:15–17, He said "Feed My sheep," a striking phrase which has a direct bearing on the right passion for souls; and after the Resurrection He said, "Go therefore and make disciples of all the nations" (Matt. 28:16–20). I want to take these three phrases as a guide for the worker in regard to this great passion for souls.

There is a telling pathos about the twenty-first chapter of John; all the disciples had forsaken the Shepherd, and Jesus said, in effect, "Now never you forsake the flock, you become broken bread and poured out wine and feed the flock." God grant we may understand that the passion for souls is not a placid, scientifically worked out thing; it compresses all the energy of heart and brain and body in one consuming drive, day and night from the beginning of life to the end—a consuming, fiery, living passion.

That was the characteristic of our Lord's life, and of the lives of all the disciples after Pentecost, and of the life of the apostle Paul.

Take first of all the phrase *fishers of men*. There are one or two significant things about that figure of speech. The early disciples were fishermen, and the Spirit of God seems to point out that their earthly employment was a parable of their divine vocation. David was a shepherd—he became the shepherd of Israel. Paul was a tentmaker; he was used by God for making people's bodies into tabernacles of the Holy Spirit. I wonder how many of you know what it is to be out all night at sea fishing? I do. Before the early dawn, about three or four in the morning, you feel so amazingly cold and so amazingly indifferent that you don't know whether you care for anything, and there is an exact counterpart of those nights in work for God. Do you know what it is to have a relationship to God so consuming, a personal, passionate devotion to Jesus Christ so powerful that it will stand you in good stead through every cold night, while you are watching and waiting to land individuals for God? It is those cold nights of waiting that are the test, cold nights of praying and of preaching, when, like Gideon's army over again, many leave and forsake and just the few are left.

What a marvelous illustration fishing is, especially fishing with the net, and Jesus Christ told the disciples He would make them fishers of men, catchers of human souls. Unless we have this divine passion for souls burning in us because of our personal love for Jesus Christ, we will quit the work before we are much older. It is an easy business to be a fisherman when you have all the enthusiasm of the catch; everybody then wants to be a fisherman. Just as everybody comes in with the shout and the Hallelujah when revival signs are abroad; but God is wanting those who through long nights, through difficult days of spiritual toil, have been trying to let down their nets to catch the fish. Oh, the skill, the patience, the gentleness, and the endurance that are needed for this passion for souls; a sense that people are perishing doesn't do it; only one thing will do it—a blazing, passionate devotion to the Lord Jesus Christ, an all-consuming passion. Then there is no night so long, no work so hard and no crowd so difficult, but that love will outlast it all.

God grant that we may see that our passion for souls springs from that on which the Moravian Mission founded its enterprise: the fifty-third chapter of Isaiah; behind every heathen face, behind every face besotted with sin they saw the face of the Son of God; behind every broken piece of earthenware they saw Jesus Christ; behind every downtrodden mass of human corruption they saw Calvary. That was the passion that was their motive. God grant we may get it back again. That is the deep, true, evangelical note for the passion for souls, the consuming passion that transfigures a man's self, that transfigures a woman's self, and makes him or her indeed wise and patient and able fishers of human souls.

Beware of the people who tell you how to fish! I know a good many people who have tried to learn how to fish from books, but they never did learn. The only way to learn how to fish is to fish! An old sea captain whom I know very well, who has been a fisherman all his days, told me he met a man who had published a book on how to catch fish. The captain took him out in his boat; they stayed out four hours, but he didn't have enough strength to put one piece of line over the boat—he was too seasick. That was the instructor of how to catch fish! Beware of the books that tell you how to catch people. Go to Calvary, and let God Almighty deal with you until you understand the meaning of the tremendous cost to our Lord Jesus Christ, and then go out to catch humans. God grant we may get away from the instructors on how to catch fish and get out into the fishing business!

Mrs. Howard Hooker pointed out in an address one day that the disciples when Jesus Christ called them were mending their nets, and she made the remark, "The majority of Christian people are always washing and mending their nets; but when Jesus Christ comes along, He tells them to launch out and let them down; it is the only way to catch fish." God grant we may see the aptness of Jesus Christ's words, "I will make you fishers of men." Is there some Sunday school teacher to whom it has been a cold, cold, year in your class, have you gone home every Sunday afternoon with a heart like lead, and have you cried to God, saying, "O God, I have prayed and asked and longed, but not one of these lives can I get for You"? God grant, if you feel like that, you may go back to Calvary again and again, until the Holy Spirit expounds to you the tremendous, passionate love of the Lord Jesus Christ.

Have you ever noticed one thing about the early disciples, that in every case the choice is the Lord's, not the disciple's? "You did not choose Me, but I chose you" (John 15:16). Jesus turned away everyone who came to Him and said, "I want to be Your disciple." Jesus Christ knows the men and women He wants. God grant that His choice may fall on every one of us, and that we may learn with patience and discipline how He is going to teach us to be patient, to be powerful, and to be passionate in His service! Never losing heart, never being discouraged, never being excited over a big catch. Many workers have rendered themselves useless to God by undue hilarity over a big revival for God. "Nevertheless do not rejoice in this, that the spirits are subject to you," said Jesus, "but rather rejoice because your names are written in heaven" (Luke 10:20). God grant we may understand that the mainspring of our passion for souls must be a personal, passionate devotion to the Lord Jesus Christ.

Then the shepherding of the flock. Read John 21: every one of the disciples had forsaken Jesus; the night got too cold, too dark, their own grief was too overwhelming, and they all forsook Him and fled. Then Jesus came to them in the upper room and imparted to them His Spirit, and then He gave them this commission: Feed My lambs; tend My sheep; feed My sheep (John 21:15–17).

Now both the fisherman's art and the shepherd's art sound poetic until you have tried them! I begin to thank God that in my boyhood and early manhood I had to take so many tries at a good many things. I did not like it at the time, but I am thankful now I had to do shepherding in the Highlands of Scotland. When you have to carry across your shoulders a dirty old wether and bring it down the mountainside, you will soon know whether shepherding is poetry or not; you will soon know whether it is not the most taxing, the most exhausting, and the most exasperating work; and Jesus used the illustration for the passion for souls. Quiet, judicious knowing how to do it won't do it; passion alone will do it. One of the grandest persons I ever knew was a sheep farmer, and he told me of his nephew whom he was trying to train as a sheep farmer (he is now a minister in Canada)—"The boy cannot learn sheep farming; it must be born in him." That used to be the old shepherd's great theory, that you could not teach one how to look after sheep unless it was born in that one. Jesus Christ drove home the very same truth to the disciples. To whom did He say, "Feed My lambs"? To Peter. Who was Peter? A very wayward sheep. Peter had not only forsaken Jesus Christ, he denied with oaths and curses he ever knew Him, and now that Peter has received the Holy Spirit and is personally, passionately devoted to Jesus Christ, do you think that anybody could have such patience with young converts as Peter? Who was it that wrote, "Shepherd the flock of God which is among you, serving as overseers, not by compulsion, but willingly"? Peter (1 Peter 5:2). Peter had marvelously learned through his own experience how to be patient, how to be tender, how to be full of grateful watchfulness over all the Lord's sheep.

But there is another aspect. When Jesus said, "Feed My sheep," He gave Peter nothing to feed them with. This is a tremendous point. You cannot nourish the flock of God unless you are rightly related to the Shepherd. You may be the mouthpiece for God's truth to the unsaved, but you cannot nourish the flock of God unless you are willing to let God use you as broken bread and poured out wine to feed His sheep. Much tried Christian worker, you are not understanding what God is putting you through; perhaps this is what He is fitting you for, to teach you how to feed His sheep, to tend the flock of God. Sunday school teacher, perhaps Jesus Christ is teaching you how He is going to make you broken bread and poured-out wine. Take some time, Christian worker, over your Bible, and see what God has to say about shepherds, about hireling shepherds. This work of feeding and tending sheep is hard work, arduous work, and love for the sheep alone will not do it; you must have a consuming love for the great Shepherd, the Lord Jesus Christ; that is the point I want to leave impressed. Love for people as human beings will never stand the strain. In order to catch them for the Lord Jesus Christ you must love Jesus Christ absolutely, beyond all others. You must have a consuming passion of love, then He will flow through you in a passion of love and yearning and draw people to Himself.

Then, lastly, "make disciples of all the nations" (Matt. 23:16–20). "Being examples to the flock" (1 Peter 5:3), said Peter. What does that mean? Be a walking, talking, living example of what you preach, in every silent moment of your life, known and unknown; bear the scrutiny of God until you prove that you are indeed an example of what He can do, and then "make disciples of all the nations." Now we come to the great, grand idea of the universal and spiritual aspect of the work of a Christian. There is no respect of persons with God, no respect of nations with God—here, there, anywhere and everywhere, wherever God likes to stir up your nest and fling you, disciple all the nations. When souls are born again into the kingdom of God the church of Christ makes a tremendous rejoicing, as it ought to make, but then what does it do? When God brings souls to you who have been brought into His kingdom by His sovereign work of grace, what have you to do? Disciple them, and the only way you can disciple them is not by making them proselytes of your views, but by teaching them to do what Jesus commanded you to do and you have done. Watch the apostle Paul's testimony: "Timothy . . . will remind you of my ways in Christ" (1 Cor. 4:17). How often the apostle Paul said when talking to his converts, "You are our glory and joy" (1 Thess. 2:20). Sunday school teacher, can you say, "God has manifested His grace in me, and if you come to the same place He will manifest it in you"? Or do you have to say, "Do as I say, but not as I do"? Before we can disciple all the nations, we ourselves must be where we want other people to be. Watch again that matchless apostle's life; the consuming, passionate agony of his soul was for the converts, not for the crowd outside; discipling is the one stamp of that mature apostle's life. "My little children, for whom I labor in birth again until Christ is formed in you" (Gal. 4:19).

Another thing: Sunday school worker, and Christian worker, and minister, you must be farther on and higher up than those you are leading, and you must be going on all the time. Now we come to the meaning of God's discipling of various workers, of His removing some workers and of putting others over the heads of others. Beware of being stationary! God grant that we may be going on with Him continually so that we can disciple all we come in contact with. When a young convert asks you a question—"Can God deliver me from the disposition of sin?"—what will you say? If you cannot answer, "Thank God, He can deliver you," then beware! God may have to remove your candlestick as a teacher, as a worker. How does the apostle Paul finish that wonderful chapter, 1 Cor. 9—"I discipline my body and bring it into subjection, lest, when I have preached to others, I myself should become disqualified" (v. 27), cast away as reprobate silver. God grant that no Christian worker may fall from the heaven of usefulness because he or she refuses to go on with God!

If you have cooled down in your spiritual life, Christian worker, has it not come about that some weeks ago, or some months ago, you were asked a question and you could not answer it, and you ought to have been able to answer it? It was a practical, pointed question about what God could do for a person's soul, or body, and you could not answer it—why? Because the side issue of your own life was not clear; and until you make that issue clear, you are left as reprobate silver. You have preached to others? Yes, and God blessed your preaching, but from the second you begin to neglect the side issues of your life, that moment God begins to leave you alone as a worker for Him. God grant you may get back again, all the avenues clearly open to Him, avenues of heart and head and body and soul, back premises and front premises, underground and overhead, and all around, clear and open to God! Then let the questions come from anywhere, questions that touch the head, questions that touch the back record, questions that touch the underneath record: "Can God restore the years the cankerworm has eaten?" "Can God alter the build of one's mind?" "Can God destroy laziness out of a person?" I was talking to an elderly minister the other day, and speaking of ministers and Christian workers generally he said, "The great defect in all branches of Christian work is laziness." The only cure for laziness is to be filled with the life of God to such an overwhelming extent that He can spend you to the last cell of your body, to the last drop of your blood, for His own glory. God grant that the consuming passion for souls for Jesus Christ's sake may get hold of us as never before!

One other thing I want you to notice with regard to this passion for souls. God will put you through many mills that are never meant for you, mills you never would be put through but that He wants to make you good bread for His little ones to eat. Christian worker, you see the meaning now of that hard place you have been in; God wants to make you bread well enough baked until you are His standard bread, and then He can break you for the feeble among the flock. What is the consuming passion in the apostle Paul's life? Devotion to the Lord Jesus Christ. "For I could wish that I myself were accursed from Christ for my brethren, my countrymen according to the flesh" (Rom. 9:3). "And I will very gladly spend and be spent out for your souls" (2 Cor. 12:15). Christian worker, have you lost out in that consuming passion? If you are getting cooled down, visit the Cross of the Lord Jesus Christ and ask the Spirit of God to give you insight into its meaning. Ask Him that you may understand it in a new way. Then go forth, and—

> Measure thy life by loss instead of gain;
> Not by wine drunk, but the wine poured forth.

The God-Approved Worker

"Be diligent to present yourself approved to God, a worker who does not need to be ashamed, rightly dividing the word of truth" (2 Timothy 2:15).

We have been dealing with the worker for the cure of souls; now I want to deal with the prevention which is better than cure. How can a man or woman become a worker approved to God? Read 1 Tim. 4:16, "Take heed to yourself, and to the doctrine." If you forget everything else, do not forget that verse. The word heed occurs also in Acts 3:5 and 20:28. It means to concentrate; to screw your mind down, fix it, limit it, curb it, confine it, rivet it on yourself and on your teaching. It is a strong word, a powerful word, a word that grips, a rousing word. That is what we have to do if we are going to be workers approved to God.

But I want you to notice first of all who is talking and who he is talking to. It is the apostle Paul talking to Timothy, or writing to Timothy, or sending a message to Timothy. Paul's method was that of apprenticeship, that is always God's method of training workers. In the old days when artists used to have apprentices, they used to put the young person in charge of mixing paints and in between doing this the younger one would watch the artist paint, and slowly, bit by bit, doing the hard work and watching the master work, would learn to "take heed." That was Paul's method. Timothy had a good mother and a godly grandmother, and he was trained spiritually in this apprentice style. If you are going to be a worker for the cure of souls, God will bring you under masters and teachers. That is the method

God always uses. He does not use anyone who is undisciplined. Thank God for every worker who was ever placed under apprenticeship!

"Take heed to yourself." That is not self-realization; it is self-preparation, and the first thing I want to notice about self-preparation is in 4:13. "Give attention to reading." The word *reading* does not mean what we understand by reading—opening a book and looking at it; it means what we understand in Scotland by expository preaching. "Listen to that kind of discourse, Timothy, read that kind of manuscript, and when you open your mouth, follow that specimen." What is expository preaching? It is not taking a text out of its setting and using it as a title; it means that the verse is taken in its setting and applied where it is meant to apply. I wonder how many workers are taking heed to their reading in this expository way. I wonder what kind of preacher you delight to listen to, what kind of book you like to read, what kind of instruction you delight to listen to? Paul tells Timothy to take heed, first of all, to this important thing. "Give attention to reading."

In order to get this more crystallized in our minds, read Neh. 8:4–5: "So Ezra the scribe stood on a platform of wood which they had made for the purpose. . . . And Ezra opened the book in the sight of all the people, for he was standing above all the people; and when he opened it, all the people stood up." That is the God-ordained method of expounding God's Word, and it is as if Paul said to Timothy, "When you read, when you listen and when you teach, remember God's time-honored method—get upon your pulpit of wood as an official." There are two kinds of official worker—the one who may become a castaway; that is what the apostle Paul dreaded—"I discipline my body and bring it into subjection, lest, when I have preached to others, I myself should become disqualified" (1 Cor. 9:27). The other kind of worker is the one who is an example of what he or she teaches.

But the point to notice here is that the person who expounds God's Word has to be seen of all the people; if one's sermons are written, let the people see they are written; if one is reading from the Bible, let the people see that one is; if one is reading someone else's sermon, let one say so. These are not trifling things, they are tremendously important things, and the word reading covers them all. "Search after that kind of preacher, Timothy, and listen to that one."

Worker for God—and I speak this to myself as well as to you—what do you fasten your mind on when you listen to a preacher, when you read a book? When Jesus Christ said "You shall love the Lord your God with all your heart," He did not stop there, He went on to say, "with all your soul, with all your mind, and with all your strength." Oh, I wish I had time, I would kindle you by telling you of some people I know who have lifted themselves out of the very gutter of ignominy and ignorance by sheer grind in the secular callings of life. Would to God we had the same stick-to-it energy in God's line! Many have I known in Scotland who worked hard day and night to attain scholarships in secular callings, and are we to be behind them? This word of the apostle Paul's is used in that connection—"Take heed," concentrate, stick at it, fix the mind on it. Give heed to reading, be careful of your self-preparation. God grant that we may be approved to God by what we build in. When Paul mentioned the matter of conversation, he said, "See that your speech is edifying"—good building-up stuff, not sanctimonious talk, but real solid stuff that makes people stronger in the Word of God, stronger in character, stronger in practical life.

Paul said to Timothy another thing, "Remind them of these things, charging them before the Lord not to strive about words to no profit, to the ruin of the hearers" (2 Tim. 2:14). And again, "Shun profane and idle babblings, for they will increase to more ungodliness. And their message will spread like cancer" (vv.

16–17). And again, "Avoid foolish and ignorant disputes, knowing that they generate strife" (v. 23). Don't argue! Don't enter into controversy at any price. Paul told Timothy not to enter into controversy at any price, and Paul was the arch-controversialist himself! Paul spent most of his days in controversy, and yet he told Timothy not to argue! But have you read Paul's method of controversy? Paul put himself with amazing courtesy and amazing insight and amazing tenderness into the place of the person he was disputing with. The reason Paul told Timothy not to argue, and the reason he tells me not to argue, and the reason he tells you not to argue, is that we argue from our own point of view. We argue not for the truth's sake, we argue to prove we are right. God grant that we may learn to take heed lest we get switched off on arguing. Is there some worker for God likely to be twisted and turned aside by battling for the faith? Let me read you some words I have jotted down in my Bible:

> Oh, the unmitigated curse of controversy! Oh, the detestable passions that corrections and contradictions kindle up to fury in the proud heart of human beings! Eschew controversy, my friends, as you would eschew the entrance to hell itself. Let them have it their way; let them talk; let them write; let them correct you; let them traduce you; let them judge and condemn you; let them slay you. Rather let the truth of God suffer itself, than that love suffer. You have not enough of the divine nature in you to be a controversialist.—*Dr. Alexander Whyte*

"Heal me," prays Augustine, again and again, "of this lust of mine of always vindicating myself."

Take heed, fix your mind, never be wheedled into controversy. Let the Spirit of God controvert. One of my greatest snares ever since I became a Christian is this very thing. I know what it means, I know the galling humiliation and agony in days that have gone by of wanting to argue the point out, and I know, possibly better than any of you, the inwardness of the point that the apostle Paul is driving at with Timothy—"Don't do it, Timothy; stop, you will damage your own soul, you will hinder the truth of God, you will bruise the souls you talk to." God grant we may fix and concentrate our minds and take heed to this! Take heed to yourself, take heed how you read, and above all don't argue. Have you learned this, Christian worker, that when people begin to discuss the baptism with the Holy Spirit, it is time you got out of the way? They have a controversy with the Holy Spirit, not with you. Sanctification is not a human term; it is God's: the baptism with the Holy Spirit is not a human conception, it is God's, and when people begin to argue on these matters, remember, worker for God, it is the Holy Spirit they are arguing with, the Word of God they are haggling about. God grant we may not hinder those who are battling their way slowly into the light.

One more thing: Paul told Timothy, "Preach the word! Be ready in season and out of season" (2 Tim. 4:2). Watch the setting of that. Timothy was fragile in body physically, Paul frequently told him how to take care of his body, and yet here the apostle told this young man who is feeble in body to preach the Word in season and out of season—what did he mean? To take every opportunity of preaching the word? He did not mean any such thing; he meant "preach the Word in season or out of season with regard to yourself, never let your bodily condition hinder your preaching." The apostle Paul was driving at laziness, heart sloth. God grant we may learn how to be ready in season and out of season, always at it, night and day, whether we feel like it or not. When you come to read deeper down between the lines in the Bible, you will find running all through it the awful curse on laziness and spiritual sloth. Has it come on you mentally, Christian worker? Then may God rouse you up to get to reading, to get to work with your pencil and notebook, in cars and out of cars, behind the counter, anywhere. God grant we may be roused up in the spiritual domain to put energy and vim into our work and never say, "I can't," "I have no time." Of course you do not, no human being worthy of the name ought to have time to give to God: you have to take it from other things until you know how God values time. Take heed to yourself, and never allow anything to produce laziness and sloth.

And lastly, "Continue in them, for in doing this you will save both yourself and those who hear you" (1 Tim. 4:16). There is the charter for the worker, to be a pattern. "Let no one despise your youth" (v. 12). Was Paul telling Timothy to stand up and say, "I know I am only a youngster, but I defy anyone to contradict me"? Paul was saying, "Do not let youth be despised in you," and then he told him, "be an example to the believers in word, in conduct, in love, in spirit, in faith, in purity." The only way youth can save itself from being despised is by the life being in keeping with the profession, the teaching backed by it, the conversation, the manner of life, the purity, the clean, vigorous, upright adulthood; not only a worker sent from God, but an example of what God can do. The baptism with the Holy Spirit and fire made the disciples the incarnation of what they taught. God grant that we may be the pattern of what we preach, that we may be workers approved to God, "rightly dividing the word of truth."

The Holy Worker

"Yet none of the rest dared join them . . . . and believers were increasingly added to the Lord" (Acts 5:13–14).

I want to end where I began, with the character of the worker. God grant we may understand the power of a holy worker for God. I don't mean a holiness worker; what we need is holy workers—there is a big difference.

"Yet none of the rest dared join them. . . . and believers were increasingly added to the Lord." Have you caught the contrast?—a holy dread and a holy discipleship, they always go together. The souls who stand true to God are those whom God's Spirit has added.

"So great fear came upon"—the crowd outside? No, "upon all the church and upon all who heard these things" (v. 12). And then a wonderful thing happened—a great benediction fell on the multitude outside, "and believers were increasingly added to the Lord, multitudes of both men and women."

I want to deal with this holy dread and holy discipleship.

"Knowing, therefore, the terror of the Lord, we persuade men" (2 Cor. 5:11). It is necessary for those of us who are workers for God to allow the Spirit of God to lift the veil sometimes and strike terror through us. We take our salvation and our sanctification too cheaply, without realizing that Jesus Christ went through the deep waters of uttermost damnation that we might have it. We read that a great fear came across the members of the early church: "So great fear came upon all the church and upon all who heard these things"—why? They realized what we have to realize, that the Pentecostal dispensation produces not only Pentecostal living people, but liars to the Holy Spirit. Look for one moment at Ananias. "But Peter said, 'Ananias, why has Satan filled your heart to lie to the Holy Spirit and keep back part of the price of the land? . . . Why have you conceived this thing in your heart?' " (Acts 5:3–4). Read the last verses of chapter 4, "Barnabas . . . . having land, sold it, and brought the money and laid it at the apostles' feet." It is probable that indirectly Barnabas was responsible for Ananias. Barnabas had done a wonderful thing and doubtless he was praised for it, and Ananias wanted to equal it. We need to live steadfastly in the presence of God so that when we are praised we don't arouse the spirit of envy, the spirit that makes a person want to do something, not because of love for God, but because he or she wants to emulate us. Let me ask you who are workers, and let me ask myself, "Why do you work for the salvation of souls? Why do you want to spend and be spent for others?" "Mrs. So-and-so does it and she is my ideal." Beware! "I watched Mr. So-and-so and I want to be like him." Beware! God grant we may see that the great need of every worker is a firsthand acquaintance with Jesus Christ which puts to death the spirit of ambition. Ambition has murder at its heart; our Lord showed His disciples that ambition is impossible in His kingdom, "Unless you . . . become as little children, you will by no means enter the kingdom of heaven" (Matt. 18:3). Our attitude is to be one of steadfast personal devotion to Jesus Christ, not measuring ourselves by ourselves, and comparing ourselves with ourselves (see 2 Cor. 10:12). Among the last words Mr. Reader Harris wrote was this phrase, "Don't imitate." That means far more than mere external imitation, it means in the deep spiritual sense what I am trying to bring before you now—don't try and do something for God because somebody else is doing it. Oh, the amount of instigation in God's work that comes along that line!

Mark one more thing. Peter said to Ananias, "You have not lied to men but to God" (Acts 5:4). Christian worker, how much time are you giving to prayer, to reading your Bible? "Oh, I am giving all the time I can." Be careful that you are not lying to the Holy Spirit. Pentecostal lying begins in this way, dragging down the intense holiness of God which keeps a person right with God in every detail of life. Let us examine ourselves the next time we say, "I do not have time," or, "I give all the time I can to the study of God's Word," "I give all the time I can to praying." God grant we may be put on the alert on these lines that we may not be found lying to the Holy Spirit. May these words come with warning and with scrutiny and bring our souls face–to–face with God.

And now, holy discipleship. "Yet none of the rest dared join them." I wonder, Christian worker, if we realize what we are doing when we ask people to give themselves to Jesus Christ, do we know what we are telling them to do? We are telling them to kill forever their right to themselves, we are telling them that they have to be holy, chaste to the last recess of their bodily lives. If ever that word needed thundering in Christian work it needs thundering today, chastity in bodily life. You cannot have holiness without a chaste physical life. Oh, the sapping of the power of God because of unchaste men and women who preach His gospel. God grant that the touch of God may startle and amaze any self-indulgent man or woman. May we remember the next time we go forth to speak for God that our bodies are the temples of the Holy Spirit. When we realize this and bind ourselves to those who realize the same truth, God will begin to do His marvels in saving individuals to Himself. So many of us are being caught up by the benedictions that fall on the crowd outside. The crowd outside will magnify the power of God, but none of those who are not right with God dare join us. If any Christian worker wants to get the strong grip of iron into his or her soul and into his or her work for God, let that worker read the Acts of the Apostles. The power of those holy workers checked impostors on the right hand and on the left. A Holy Spirit movement always brings impostors, parasites, by the legion. The only safeguard for the Christian worker is, "Holiness to the Lord" (Exod. 28:36). If we are living rightly with God, living holy lives in secret and in public, God puts a wall of fire round about us. Beware of calling anything holiness that is only winsome and sweet to the world. God grant we may never lose the touch of God that produces the holy dread.

Now we come to our last point. This holy discipleship will result in multitudes being added to the Lord. "And believers were increasingly added to the Lord, multitudes of both men and women." Is not that what we want, multitudes added to the Lord? How is it to be done? By captivating addresses? Mrs. Howard Hooker reminded me the other night when speaking of her father, that his preaching was always on the line of sanctification; a great many people could not stand it and consequently went away. It has always been the same and always will be. When the holiness of God is manifested in human lives and in preaching (and the two go together), these two things happen: a great number dare not join themselves, and multitudes are added to the Lord. Never think that the blessing and benediction of God on the outside crowd is all. It is a mere fringe. Men and women are blessed, their bodies are healed, devils are turned out; but the point is that multitudes of those who believe are added to the Lord. God grant that we may stand steadfastly true to Him and live this holy life. As we go forth tonight, let us remember Jesus Christ's commission, "All authority has been given to Me in heaven and on earth. Go therefore and make disciples of all the nations" (Matt. 28:18–19). As we examine our hearts before God, let us renew our covenant with Him.

Note to the Reader

The publisher invites you to share your response to the message of this book by writing Discovery House Publishers, P. O. Box 3566, Grand Rapids, MI 49501, U.S.A. or by calling 1-800-653-8333. For information about other Discovery House publications, contact us at the same address and phone number.

The following Oswald Chambers books are also available from Discovery House Publishers: